CONTENTS

Chapter 1: Background

1.1 Introduction

Entertainment is a form of activity that aims to capture and retain the interest of an audience, usually giving pleasure or delight. It is an inherent element of life that has evolved over time. The Ancient Egyptians played board games and sports, hunted, celebrated festivals and engaged in storytelling for entertainment. The Romans entertained themselves by watching gladiators battle to the death.

Various new forms of entertainment have emerged over the years, often broadly stemming from a previous form, a subsect so to speak. An example of this is the various forms of sport activities we see today. At this present day, there are over 8000 forms of sport around the world, with around 440 being internationally recognised. The 20th Century could be considered the era of sports, with activities like football and boxing being huge entertainment activities.

Entertainment is subjective and changes according to societies perception on entertainment. Gladiators fighting to the death would not be generally acceptable in society today. Going further, sport popularity and perception are often segmented regionally. For example, NFL is huge in North America whereas in Europe, football is the dominant sport.

Towards the end of the 20th century, the gaming industry has established itself on a global scale, making real strides as an entertainment activity, particularly as technology has developed further. It is apparent that society has shifted towards a gaming culture, resulting in the industry becoming a multi-billion-pound segment within the entertainment market, over a few decades.

Within this gaming industry, a niche subsect has formed and evolved on a global scale. This niche aspect of the gaming industry is known as esports or competitive gaming. Think of it as the baby of video gaming and sports. We are, unquestionably, in the 'video gaming sports' (or 'esports') era in history.

My grandparents never played a single video game in their whole lives. They often had no time to play and there was no real availability of games. My parents did play video games to some degree, albeit Pac-Man and Space Invaders, but primarily played traditional sports. From my observations, it appears that from generation to generation, there is more exposure to games, in some form or another.

I myself was born in the 90s and fortunately grew up around both games and sports. I played and watched various sports, particularly football and cricket. I continue to play football on a regular basis and have been an Arsenal fan for over fifteen years. I also am an avid gamer. In terms of consoles, I have been a Playstation fan from the PS1 to the PS4. Additionally, I had a Gameboy where I used to 'Catch 'em all' on Pokémon. Even at school, we used to play games on websites like Miniclip and have Unreal Tournament competitions. I have also played many other PC games with friends over the years, including Runescape and the Warcraft series.

The point is that I have played a vast array of games over the years and the important thing to note is that the games I enjoyed the most have been ones that I could play competitively. Whether it was playing friends or others online, I wanted to be the best. It is this inherent competitive element in our DNA that has enabled esports to establish itself as a 'one to watch' industry.

Despite my avid gaming, I only became aware of the esports movement around three years ago. Following the initial idea for my business, I decided to do some research to see whether there was a market. It was then that I came across esports. I could not believe I had not heard of this earlier. Although, technically esports has been around for over twenty years, it is only in the last five that it has really taken off.

Since becoming aware of esports, I have put a significant dent into my 'ten thousand hours' to learn as much as I can about the complex industry. I have watched the industry with an intent eye for the last three years as I acquired my law degree at University.

Having graduated July 2017, I have pushed myself even further to expand my knowledge within the esports space. I have published several articles and have even discussed esports sponsorship on a panel at a conference in London recently. Despite this, I would not say I am an expert within this dynamic, complex and vast industry. The industry will constantly change as the industry matures, so continual development within the field is crucial and hence why I will update the book on a yearly basis.

This book aims to codify the knowledge and ideas I have developed over the years in relation to esports. This includes the key opportunities in the market, factors that are and will be the driving factors for growth and other pertinent information that would be useful for anyone wishing to delve into esports, as I am. I aim to provide a comprehensive guide to anyone who wishes to know more about the next billion-dollar industry.

1.2 What are Esports?

Esports or electronic sports are a form of competition that is facilitated by electronic systems, particularly video gaming. It is essentially a term that is used to describe playing games competitively. Just like football players play football together, esports players play video games together. A specific game played for a sport would be termed an esport (singular).

With the rise of the gaming industry, it is only natural that we have seen a competitive gaming scene grow concurrently. I think it would be naive to think that a competitive segment would not also rise from the flames of the global phenomenon of the gaming industry.

Esports are much like its traditional real-life sports brethren in their nature, but the main distinction is that esports are generally engaged online. Most commonly, esports takes the form of organised video game competitions, normally between professional players. It typically involves team-based gaming as a spectator sport, with ranked matches, although there are individual esports competitions. There are huge tournaments all over the world that take place in big arenas with vast crowds and colossal prize pools.

Esports is essentially a start-up industry with dozens of start-ups within it. As it entails gaming competitively, there are a vast number of titles that could be played at a competitive level. Increased accessibility to devices that enable gaming has further increased the scope of esports. Think about how many games you can play on your console, pc or even mobile. All it takes is a competitive element of the game for it to potentially sprout out as an esport. As the potential of the industry is realised, more game publishers will develop their games with esports in mind.

1.3 History of Esports

Some of the earliest well-known video games, such as Pong in the '70s, were in fact competitive. During the 1970s and 1980s, video game players began featuring in popular magazines. One of the most well-known classic arcade game players, Billy Mitchell, set several high score records for six games. As a result, he featured in the 1985 Issue of the Guinness Book of World Records. Televised esport events also aired during this period, such as the American show Starcade (1982-1984). On this show, contestants would attempt to beat each other's high scores on an arcade game.

The earliest video game competition took place in 1972 at Stanford University for the game Spacewar. The competition was called the 'Intergalactic Spacewar Olympics', where players were pitted against each other in an arena-style format. Competitors played as one of five different ships, avoiding hazards and gravitational pulls, whilst trying to torpedo enemies. Around 24 players gathered to compete in the five-man free-for-all and team competition for a chance to win a year's subscription to Rolling Stone.

By 1980, the first large-scale recorded video game competition was held by Atari, called the Space Invaders Championship. This competition attracted more than 10,000 participants across the US who attempted to record the highest score, establishing competitive gaming as a mainstream hobby. In 1981, Twin Galaxies (a gaming world record organisation) formed and began keeping track of top players' scores in titles like Donkey Kong and Space Invaders. They continue to run to this day.

From the 1990s onwards, the industry benefitted from increased internet connectivity and improved technology, particularly for PC games. This benefitted esports tremendously and is the period that video gaming took great strides. More competitive games emerged, such as Super Street Fighter II and Doom. Large esport tournaments were also held during this period, such as the 1990 and 1994 Nintendo World Championships which toured across the United States. Blockbuster video also ran their own World Game Championship in the early 90s where citizens from the USA, Canada, UK, Australia and Chile were eligible to compete.

By the late 90s, the number of tournaments started to proliferate. Competitions that were established in this period include: QuakeCon, Professional Gamers League (PGL) and Cyberathlete Professional League (CPL).

QuakeCon is a yearly convention that was founded in 1996 which included a large bring-your-own-computer (BYOC) competitive tournament held every year in Texas, USA.

Twenty-one years later, the event is still running, with thousands of gamers from all over the world in attendance.

The Professional Gamers League (PGL) was founded in 1997 and was one of the first professional gaming esport leagues, run by Total Entertainment Network (TEN) and sponsored by the multinational, NASDAQ listed, company AMD Inc. The first professional tournament they hosted was for StarCraft, in which they received sponsorship from Microsoft, Nvidia, and Levi Strauss & Co, raising over $1.2 million in sponsorship money. It continues to run in the present day, with competitions held for a variety of games including Counter-Strike, Dota-2 and Hearthstone.

The Cyberathlete Professional League (CPL) was also founded in 1997, pioneering professional video game tournaments. Esports professionals began to make a name for themselves through the CPL, such as Johnathan Wendel.

Johnathan, known as 'Fatal1ty', has reportedly earned around half a million US dollars in prizes during his esports career, signed several sponsorship deals and even created his own brand of gaming accessories. The CPL hosted competitions for a variety of games, including Counter-Strike, Quake and Warcraft up until around 2007. From 2007 onwards, the range of games played at the CPL increased in number, including popular games such as League of Legends and StarCraft II.

In 1999, new shooting games emerged such as Unreal Tournament and Counter Strike. The Counter Strike series has become one of the world's most popular esports games. By the 21st century, Multiplayer Online Battle Arena (MOBA) games entered the scene and became a real hit. This genre of games often pits two teams against each other, blending strategy and RPG elements together. Each player controls a single character, who can level up, buy new items to get stronger and work with teammates to defeat the enemy team. Two of the most popular MOBA games, League of Legends and Dota 2, have gained enormous followings. Today, League of Legends has around 100 million active players.

These two MOBA games have become a staple in the competitive gaming scene. Concurrently, in the 21st century, esports has grown tremendously in terms of both viewership and prize money. Although large esports tournaments were established before the 21st century, the number and scope of the tournaments have increased significantly. Today, esports is bigger than ever.

The growth of esports could be attributed to many driving factors, including; increase increased internet connectivity, improvement in technology, increase variety of games and popularity of gaming in society. I will evaluate the different driving factors for the growth of the industry in the next section.

1.4 Driving Factors

There are many factors that could be attributable to driving the growth of the esports industry forward. In this section, I will outline the key driving factors that I believe have been instrumental in the industries growth over the years.

Firstly, improved internet connectivity has allowed esports to truly flourish through online play. The ability for gamers to compete in tournaments from the comfort of their own home is a factor that has undoubtedly propelled the industry forward. Players now can engage and play with fellow gamers online, irrespective of geographical location, increasing the convenience and sphere of influence of competitions. When online play was first introduced, there was an annoying lag time and the internet connection was temperamental, which would make playing online games frustrating. Now, with improvements to internet connectivity, online play is much improved. Online play and improved internet connectivity have provided gamers with the opportunity to connect with other like-minded gamers from all over the world. In turn, this has allowed gaming to become truly global and a core aspect of our culture.

Secondly, technology has improved by leaps and bounds over the years and it is significantly apparent in the gaming industry. If you compare gaming today with the ancient gaming industry of twenty years ago, it would be very difficult to find the resemblance. There are many examples of how the improvement in technology has driven the growth of esports, such as Artificial Intelligence. Future technologies, such as Virtual Reality, will also thrust the gaming industry to new heights.

Moreover, the utilisation of technology by the esports audience has enabled vast content consumption. There are over 4000 esports tournaments a year for the top titles, which means there is a lot of content for fans. The audience's technical aptitude grows at a rapid rate due to the necessities of playing video games, watching the games and communicating with the community. In turn, this consumption has led to exponential growth in community building and development within the industry. Gamers are building e-communities through websites and clans/guilds/groups, creating long distance friendships in the process.

The current ecosystem provides for people, with similar interest, to quickly find one another and group up to share esports content. The fans understand their game, the stats, the best players, items and their potential, strategies and so on. They often share this knowledge through various platforms, such as social media, creating a cohesive community that only looks to expand further and cement gaming culture within our society.

Thirdly, the popularity and emergence of online streaming services have also been fundamental in driving the growth of the industry, and are the most common method of watching esport tournaments. Twitch, an online streaming platform launched in 2011, routinely streams popular esports competitions. As of July 2017, Twitch has had over 241 billion minutes of gaming content livestreamed, 10 million daily active users and over 100+ million unique monthly users. It is clear from these figures that digital streaming platforms are spearheading the growth of the industry.

Fourthly, there has been an increased popularity of gaming in society, particularly among the youth. Naturally, within this gaming culture, competitive elements have arisen as gamers aim to have the ultimate bragging rights. A gaming society that loves competition is a natural ingredient for driving the growth of the esports industry forward. This is reflected in the increased popularity for televised and streaming of esports. Other gamers watch top players of their chosen game to try and learn from the best, as well as feeding their entertainment cravings. Traditional sports organisations, celebrities and non-endemic brands have realised that there is a shift to a gaming society and have begun getting into the space.

Fifthly, increased availability of platforms and devices to play games have been a driving force for the gaming industry and esports. From the development of computers all the way to the present day, there has been a significant increase in the number of devices that can be used to play games.

Additionally, the availability of these platforms has increased significantly around the world. The number of people with access to computers, mobile phones, PS4's and Xbox's are truly staggering. According to the United Nations Agency that oversees international communication, there are more than 3.7 billion people now using the internet. According to Business Insider, Sony have sold over 60 million PS4 consoles and Microsoft have sold approximately 26 million Xbox One consoles.

Sixthly, video game publishers are also embracing the esports potential of their products. Take Nintendo for example, hosting the Wii Games Summer 2010: a one-month tournament with over 400,000 participants. Halo was revived as an esport with the creation of the Halo Championship

Series in 2014, with a prize pool of $50,000. Additionally, both Blizzard and Riot Games have their own collegiate outreach programmes with their North America Collegiate Championship. Moreover, game publishers are now taking esports into consideration when updating and developing games. They are incorporating esports into their game clients and other communication channels. This approach by game publishers has provided a bespoke approach to the esports market, catering to the target audience.

Lastly, as the industry has grown, there has been an influx of sponsorships and a dramatic increase in prize money. With the hype around the esports industry and the earning potential, it is no wander that the industry is attracting vast amounts of new fans and participants.

Esports may not be something new, but has become increasingly and successfully attractive to the public. All these different elements, and more, are fuelling the

exponential growth of the esports industry. The rise of social

media, live streaming and extended distribution options for

broadcast have enabled esports to truly breakdown

geographical barriers in a way that traditional sports have

often struggled with. Esports is a hugely complex market and

it would be incorrect to pin the success of the industry on one

individual factor. It is the concoction of factors that I have

highlighted in this section that have been integral in driving

the esports industry forward.

Chapter 2: Esports Market Economics

2.1 Overview of The Market

As you delve into the esports market, it is apparent that the industry has come a long way and has a huge potential for growth.

Due to its globalised and online nature, viewership for esports is significant, making it comparable to traditional sports. Additionally, the viewership is increasing as time goes on, not diminishing. It is suggested that esports will have more viewers than NFL Football by 2020. The industry has been described as an 'advertising goldmine', supported by the fans spending habits.

Nearly every big esports tournament is streamed free to Twitch. This platform allows people to watch their favourite team or individual players while chatting with other spectators. Some watch for pure entertainment, others watch to learn from the best and apply that knowledge to their own games.

As online viewership within esports has grown, the scope of events and physical viewership of esports events has also increased. An example of this can be seen by the annual League of Legends World Championship. In 2013, the League of Legends World Championship was held in a sold-out Staples Center with approximately 19,000 attendees. Following from this, the League of Legends 2014 World Championship in South Korea had 40,000 fans in attendance and even featured the band Imagine Dragons!

With these past events attracting crowds comparable to live established sport games, professional sport franchise owners will be aware that esports can provide an avenue to fill arenas.

As the market continues to grow, owners would benefit from events that can fill up their arenas when games are not on.

Football clubs such as Manchester City have started signing FIFA stars who are players of the virtual game, rather than the real thing. Other clubs, such as Paris Saint-Germain (PSG), have signed up a whole squad of players in a variety of esports.

The thinking is simple for these clubs: digital gaming is where the next generation of fans will come from. Often, a young person's first interaction with a professional football club is through the FIFA game, and so esports are a vast reservoir of future income. Additionally, esports will allows clubs to raise their global profile. It will allow clubs to generate new fans of the brand, tapping into US and Asian markets, who may not necessarily be fans of football.

A variety of large companies are also paying attention to esports, primarily due to the desirable demographics of the audience and the clear potential of the industry. In 2014, Amazon purchased the online streaming provider Twitch for $1 Billion. In the following year, Modern Times Group, a Swedish based media company, purchased Turtle Entertainment (the holding company for ESL) for $87 Million. The Canadian entertainment company Cineplex spent $15 million in the same year to acquire an esports company and create a new gaming league that will take place in its theatres. Although esports might not match or surpass traditional sports any time soon, its potential business value is clearly too significant to ignore.

In Britain, we are just starting out on the esports road, relatively speaking. Traditional sport still dominates, but every day new evidence of change emerges. BT Sport broadcasted the FIFA 17 Ultimate Team Championship Series in the UK for the first time this year. Last month, Tottenham Hotspur announced their new ground will host live eSports matches, with potential crowds of 50,000 and revenue of up to £3m a match. It is only a matter of time before UK catches the esports fever, especially considering that UK gamers spent almost £3.3 billion on video games in 2016, according to NewZoo.

2.2 Market Size & Growth Rate

Looking at the global revenue of esports in NewZoo's reports over the last few years demonstrates the industries growth rate and potential. In 2015, the global revenue for esports was $325 million. The following year, the global revenue increased by 51.7% to $493 million. The 2017 global revenue for esports will amount to $696 million, a 41.3% increase from 2016. NewZoo forecast the global revenue for esports to increase to around $1.5 billion by 2020, as brand investment doubles.

NewZoo also posits that the global awareness of esports will reach approximately 1.3 billion this year, up from 1.1 billion in 2016. Awareness is forecasted to approach 1.8 billion by 2020. The market is already at a colossal stage despite having significant room to grow. Esports is expected to rival major league sports in the immediate future.

2.3 Audience Profile

The NewZoo report states that the global esports audience has increased by about 19% from 2016, reaching 385 million this year. This is made up of 191 million esports enthusiasts and a further 194 million occasional viewers. The number of esports participants will reach 58.4 million this year, up from 49.8

million in 2016. To demonstrate the size of this market, if this audience was classified as a country, it would be the third largest according to population.

By 2020, the global esports audience will be well over 500 million, with the number esports enthusiasts expected to grow to approximately 286 million. The key drivers for the esports audience growth includes the rise of streaming platforms, new franchises like FIFA and Overwatch joining the scene and growth in emerging regions.

The esports audience skews young and male, with half of them aged between 21-35 and over 71% men. Majority of these are in full time employment and have a decent income. Their demographics make them a very desirable target group for different parties, especially big brands. Particularly as digital natives are more likely to be consuming content online than through traditional media outlets.

There is a large technical aptitude to the esports audience, which consists of Generation Y (including Millennials) and Generation Z. This demographic like skill-based entertainment, preferably through digital means. Esports has the potential to offer them this type of experience.

Pro-players and viewers predominantly trends to a young, male demographic on a global scale, which should be very attractive to advertisers and sponsors.

2.4 Market Segmentation

The esports market can be segmented in a variety of ways. Esports market segments can be-identified by genre, the game title, platforms used, key players, revenue source and based on location.

The most obvious segment within esports is within genres and games. Esports is composed of different genre of games, such as Multiplayer Online Battle Arena (MOBA), First-Person Shooters (FPS) and Sports games. Although there will often be some overlap, the market for some games and genre segments would not be the same for others. Take shooting games and sports games for example. Some, like myself, will play games in both genres, such as Call of Duty and FIFA. Others, however, may only play games in one of the genres.

As shown by the Nielsen report, the market is further segmented according to the platforms utilised to play games. Gamers have been spoilt for choice in the present day with a whole host of platforms that can be played on. The most popular platforms would be the PC, PS4 and the Xbox One.

The market is also segmented according to the key players in the esports industry. The 'key player' segments include; fans, players, teams, organisations, game publishers, event producers, associations and communities.

In relation to revenue source within the esports landscape, the market can be categorised into; sponsorships, advertising, merchandising, ticket sales, esports betting, fantasy esports, prize pools and media rights, to name a few.

Geographically, the esports market is segmented by regions. Within different regions, the size of the esports market and the popularity of games differs. Take sports games for example. In the US, the most popular sports game is Madden, whereas in Europe it is FIFA.

2.5 Regional Analysis

Esports is at different stages of development across the globe. While esports have long been biggest in Asia, particularly South-Korea, North American and European markets are growing exponentially. It is important to note that there are key differences in the esports markets on a regional level. This is considered further in the Nielsen Report chapter.

NewZoo's 2017 esports report highlights the present size of the esports market, in terms of revenue, in the different regions.

The Asian esports market is one of the most established and largest regions. According to NewZoo, the global revenue for esports within the Asian market is around $328 million, with the Chinese market reaching around $104.4 million. Around 11.1 billion esport videos were streamed in 2016 in China. 57% of esport viewers come from China, with at least 6 million university students taking part.

The 2022 Asian Games, to be hosted in the Chinese city of Hangzhou, home of online retail giant Alibaba, will include esports as a medal event.

North America is also dominant region in terms of numbers of gamers and revenue generated in the esports market. The North American esports market was forecasted by NewZoo to reach $257.5 million in 2017.

About 20 US universities have made esports official varsity programmes. In 2016, Japan surprised many by agreeing to allow visiting esports tournament participants to enter the country on visas normally reserved for athletes.

The European market is estimated to generate a global esports market revenue of around $269 million. Esports revenue within Europe is mainly generated from Western countries, like Germany and France.

2.6 Revenue Streams

The key revenue streams within esports include; sponsorships, advertising, merchandising, ticket sales, media rights, prize pools, esports betting and fantasy esports.

According to NewZoo's report, the revenue breakdown according to source is as follows:

- Sponsorship - $266.3 million (+57.7% increase)

- Advertising - $155.3 million (+21% increase)

- Game Publisher Fees - $115.8 million (+17.9% increase)

- Media Rights - $95.2 million (+81.5% increase)

- Merchandise & Tickets - $63.7 million (+42.4% increase)

Sports investors find esports compelling because of the industry's ability to tap into the five main revenue streams:

Sponsorships, Advertising, Merchandise, Tickets and Media Rights. The most lucrative revenue streams, according to NewZoo, are sponsorships and advertising. Sponsorship and advertising account for 60% of the total global esports revenue from the five main streams. This can be attributed to many new brands and advertisers entering the space. The other revenue streams, such as merchandising and ticket sales, are huge untapped markets. They have huge potential to grow as the industry matures and other issues are addressed.

Additionally, it is important to note that the revenue does not stop with the five main sources. There is revenue generated as the industry converges established industries and through other distinct sources, such as esports betting and fantasy sites.

2.7 Direct Advertising & Sponsorship

The esports landscape has been compared to the Wild-West, however, if a marketer can navigate through this space there would be substantial rewards. Gamers have shown loyalty to brands that do it right as it is this investment from celebrities, endemic and non-endemic brands that has fuelled the exponential growth of the esports industry.

The digital age and online advertising has changed remarkably over the years. Native advertisements and banner advertisements prevailed over the internet in the 2000s. Now, they are despised and are the least effective according to the CPM (cost per mile), how much the ads are looked at and clicked on. As a result, methods of marketing have evolved and become more creative. The internet user is now less ok with invasive ads and ad block rates are at an all-time high.

As a result, traditional forms of marketing are now becoming less effective.

Esports represents a huge untapped market for advertisers. NewZoo, a research company, predicts that brands will invest more than $1 billion in esports advertising by 2020.

If you are seeking to secure sponsorship as a team, player or event – utilising and extrapolating data from previous events hosted, along with reasonable predictions to back it up would be beneficial. For example, approaching a sponsor and informing them that you have had 5000 viewers for your last tournament with minimal investment. Then you can predict, reasonably, how much viewers you can get with some capital. This number will be the exposure of the sponsor's product or service. Let's say you predict that with a £5,000 sponsorship, you can get 15000 core viewers at your next event. That means for every £1 the sponsor spends, their brand gets exposed to 3 viewers. Framing your proposal in this manner puts the proposal into a much better perspective for the sponsor.

Depending on what product or service the sponsor is selling, you can then work out what their return on investment would be. Using a £10 product as an example, it would be clear that you would only need 500 viewers to purchase the sponsor's product to recuperate their investment. That is one in every thirty viewers making a purchase.

Direct Advertising

Advertisements are defined by the Advertising Association of the UK as messages paid for by those who send them, which are intended to inform or influence people who receive them. These messages can take the form of various platforms, including television, radio, internet, events, sponsorships, clothes, sounds, visuals and even people (endorsements).

As traditional forms of advertising have become less effective, brands are looking for innovative ways to reach their target audience. Esports provides brands with a platform to reach their target audience and have a significant return on investment, if done right.

Sponsorship

Many events and organisations use sponsorship to offer more exciting programs and to help cover rising costs. In turn, sponsorship allows the sponsor to reach specifically targeted niche markets without any waste. According to Nielsen Market Intelligence, since the start of 2016, there has been over 600 esports sponsorship agreements.

Sponsorship is the financial or in-kind support of an activity that is primarily used to reach specific business goals. According to IEG's Complete Guide to Sponsorship, "Sponsorship should not be confused with advertising. Advertising is considered a quantitative medium, whereas sponsorship is considered a qualitative medium. It promotes a company in association with the sponsee." Sponsorship and brand partnership have been fundamental in helping accelerate the growth of esports globally.

Sponsorship is a powerful marketing tool that is a powerful complement to other marketing programs. Esports sponsorship provides the brands with significant opportunities for distinct marketing, whilst showing support to the player, organisation or team as well as the industry. This often results in the target market perceiving the sponsorship in a positive way. Brands are provided with the prospect of broadening their competitive advantage by increasing their credibility, image and prestige.

Below are a few of the benefits a brand can get from Sponsorships:

- Return on Investment: The investment from the sponsor can reap huge rewards for both parties.

- Enhanced Image: Sponsoring events that appeal to their target market are likely to shape buying attitudes and have a dramatic effect on customer relations. The audience will see the sponsor in a positive light for adding value to esports.

- Driving Sales: Sponsors can showcase their product and services. Often food & beverage companies use sponsorship to encourage sampling and sales. Other companies can use a 'causal strategy', like American Express with their 'Charge Against Hunger' campaign where they donated to needy causes. Consequently, this campaign provided a significant rise in sales volume.

- Enhanced Positive Exposure: Positive publicity results in heightened visibility of the company's products and services. Target audiences often perceive sponsorship in a positive way, as the sponsorship often allows more or better activities to take place. Various media platforms covering the event will often have sponsors names and/or photos. Therefore, sponsorship can generate media coverage that might not have been available otherwise.

- Differentiation from Competitors: This is particularly the case with exclusive sponsorships. The company have an opportunity to stand out from the competition, which is particularly helpful if the competition has a larger Ad budget. It essentially is a powerful tool that smaller companies can use to combat industry giants.

- Providing 'Good Corporate Citizen' Status: Sponsorship allows companies to be perceived as a 'good neighbour'. By supporting the community and contributing to the economic development of esports, the sponsor would gain enormous goodwill. This has been shown in the esports industry as fans favour sponsors providing value.

To some extent, sponsorship allows for exposure in an audience that would not be reached otherwise. Many of the early sponsors had existing ties to the gaming industry (endemic brands), such as PC manufacturers (such as Intel) and peripherals makers such as Logitech. Now, however, more traditional non-endemic brands are starting to join in.

Some examples include, Vodafone sponsoring the Spanish team G2 Esports and the razor brand Gillette, which sponsored the ESL's Intel Extreme Masters in Poland this year. The Team Liquid franchise are sponsored by gambling brand PokerStars, among others.

Three-time NBA champion with the Los Angeles Lakers, Rick Fox, launched his own esports franchise last year. He believes that potential sponsors are showing increasing levels of interest in competitive video gaming. Fox believes that the brands, leaders and early adopters that build a presence in esports now will be able to carve out opportunities for themselves and consequently will be well set for the future.

When deciding to enter the esports space as a sponsor, it is important to create a solid strategy for activation. It needs to make sense and done for the right reasons. Additionally, before sponsoring, the sponsor must feel that the event or organisation will be successful. This confidence can be achieved through the sponsee's proven track record, good prospects and general alignment with the sponsor's brand and business objectives.

The entity receiving the sponsorship also stands to benefit enormously from both financial support and other forms of backing from an established partner, provided that the agreement, partnership and activation is done right.

Chapter 3: The Esports Industry

This chapter will focus on the industry itself, particularly the different components and players that make up esports presently. As you will see from this chapter, the esports industry is hugely complex because of the number of key players within the space.

3.1 Esport Genres

Within the gaming industry, there are several genres that games can fall under. These different genres appeal to different demographics, which is what makes esports so lucrative and exciting. Often, games can overlap into more than one genre. Below are some of the top esport genres.

Multiplayer Online Battle Arena (MOBA) – Games include League of Legends and Dota-2

This genre is also known as Action Real-Time Strategy (ARTS). The genre is often team based games, where the players characters usually have various abilities and advantages that improve over the course of the game. This genre is a fusion of Action, Role-Playing and Real-Time Strategy games. This genre has become a staple of the emerging esports scene, and concurrently is the most popular in terms of participation and viewership. The world is MOBA mad, with developers around the world trying to get their slice of the battle arena pie.

MOBA games often require a great deal of intelligence. Studies that have been conducted to measure the connection between intelligence and video game performance, focussing on MOBA games. Essentially, five players would face off against each other, with the goal usually to take over the other team's base. Each player controls a single avatar that can be any one of a number of characters with unique abilities and moves. Communication is key between the players in a team, so they can engage in strategy in order to win the game. Games in this genre require players to have a strong memory and a deep understanding of tactic and strategy in order to win.

First-Person Shooters (FPS) – Games include Counter Strike, Call of Duty, Overwatch

First-Person Shooters are video games that are centred in a first-person perspective, often around firearms and other weapon-based combat. The genre shares similarities with shooter games and so falls under the heading of action games. Games in this genre are often fast paced with bloody firefights.

Shooting games have become widely successful as a game genre, accounting for a huge portion of video game sales. The Call of Duty franchise, for example, has had more than 175 million sales across all titles.

Fighting Games – Games include Street Fighter, Tekken and Mortal Kombat

This genre usually consists of gamers controlling an on-screen character, engaging in close combat with the opponent. These games often involve violent and exaggerated attacks against opponents. Hand to hand combat is often emphasised, with some ranged and melee weapons often featuring.

Fighting games were the dominating genre in the 1990s but have faced a general decline. Even popular franchises that have been release post-1990s have not attained the popularity of earlier fighting games.

Real-Time Strategy (RTS) – Games include StarCraft and Warcraft

This game genre often entails a multiple unit selection game, where multiple game characters can be selected to perform different tasks, as opposed to selecting only one. The real-time element has evolved from the turn based systems seen previously.

Sports Games – Games include FIFA, Madden and NBA 2k

The sport game genres usually simulates traditional sports, such as football. Within this genre, gamers can play their favourite traditional sports and utilise their favourite players or teams. One of the best-selling series in this genre is the FIFA video game series.

The sport genre emerged early in the history of video games, with titles like Pong in the '70s. Due to the genres nature, it remains popular today.

Racing Games – Games include Trackmania, iRacing and Forza

Games within the racing genre consist of gamers competing against time or an opponent, using some means of transportation. Racing games can be considered in the category of sports as well.

3.2 Esport Titles

Within the gaming industry, there are a vast number of games that could be played at a competitive level, but only a handful are popular esport titles. As you will see from this section, the most popular esport titles are hugely complex and require a good understanding of the game. The mechanics of the game needs to be understood and strategies implemented. Additionally, considering many of the titles involve team-based esports competitions, there is a high degree of teamwork required as well.

It is also worth noting that esport titles come and go. Many popular esport titles in the '90s are no longer at the top of the scale, in terms of viewership and participation. This section should provide an insight into what makes titles hugely popular in the present landscape of the esports industry.

League of Legends (LoL)

League of Legends is a multiplayer online battle arena (MOBA) video game, developed and published by Riot Games, for Microsoft Windows and MacOS. The game employs a freemium model, funded by microtransactions to purchase champions, champion skins, ward skins and certain multi-game boosts.

The hugely popular game was released in 2009 and has grown to over one hundred million active players each month. LoL has among the largest footprint of any game in online streaming media communities such as YouTube and Twitch. The games popularity has led to expansion into merchandise (toys, accessories, apparels) and the tie-ins to other media such as music videos, web series, documentaries and books.

In LoL, gamers play the role of an unseen 'summoner' who controls a 'champion' with unique abilities. They can battle against a team of other players or computer controlled champions. There are many distinct game modes with goals such as destroying the opposing team's 'nexus' – a structure that lies at the heart of the base protected by defensive structures.

The champions start off relatively weak but increase in strength as they acquire items and experience over the course of the game. As of August 2017, there are currently 138 champions in LoL. The most important distinction between the champions are in the type of damage that they deal.

Physical damage is resisted by the armour stat and magical damage is resisted by the magic resistance stat. Some champions can deal a combination of both and can choose which damage type to emphasise. Furthermore, item choice plays a fundamental role in a champions character. The official Riot classification of the champions are as follows:

1) Marksman – Ranged champions that usually deal physical damage. These champions are usually high damage per second (DPS) as they focus on sustained long-term damage as opposed to burst. They tend to have a weak defence.

2) Mage – Magical champions that deal magic damage and support skills. The mage champions are hugely diverse as some focus on killing a single champion from range very quickly while others specialise in area of effect damage to multiple targets. They tend to have weak defence and mobility.

3) Assassin – Melee champion that usual deals physical damage. These champions tend to have excellent mobility but a weak defence.

4) Tank – These champions are hard to kill and soak up damage for their team. They also have useful 'crowd control' capabilities to distract or disable enemies, or force the enemy to attack them first. In exchange for these strengths, the tank usually deals less damage.

5) Fighter – With a blend of attributes from a damage dealer and tank, these champions combine moderate survivability with damage. This champion is a

common choice for close-range melee fighters as they need to be able to survive long enough to close in on their target.

6) Support – These champions have skills that are meant to directly aid the rest of the team. By utilising the ability to heal, buff allies and debuff enemies these champions are essential for most teams.

As you can see, this title is hugely complex with a vast array of variables. The League is active and widespread within the esports scene with over 1900 tournaments completed and over $48 million awarded in prizes.

Riot Games organise the League Championship Series (LCS) in Europe and North America, consisting of ten professional teams in each continent. Similar competitions also exist in the Asian market; including League of Legends Pro League LPL (China), League of Legends Championship Korea LCK

(South Korea), League of Legends Master Series LMS
(Taiwan) and the Garena Premier League GPL (Southeast
Asia). These regional competitions conclude with the annual
World Championship. The 2016 World Championship had 43
million unique viewers and a total prize pool of over $6
million.

More recently, the 2017 League of Legends World
Championship took place at a completely sold-out Bird's Nest
Stadium in Beijing (around 40,000+ fans). An augmented
reality dragon (modelled after the in-game Elder Drake)
soared around the Olympic arena halfway through the
performance, with a giant Summoner's Cup rising from the
grounds of the stadium at the same time. The overall
performances of the Championship ceremony received
widespread praises.

Dota-2

Dota-2 is another free to play MOBA game, developed and published by Valve Corporation in 2013. The esports juggernaut is the sequel to the Defence of the Ancients (Dota). Interestingly, there are 132 heroes in Dota but currently 115 in the sequel. Valve appear to be bringing all the heroes over to Dota-2 slowly.

In this game, players independently control a powerful hero, who have unique abilities and differing styles of play. The heroes often have a distinct role that defines how they are to be used on the battlefield, although many heroes can perform multiple roles. Dota-2 heroes are divided into three categories: Strength, Agility and Intelligent.

During a match, two teams select their individual heroes that collect experience points and gold, which they can use to purchase items, to grow stronger. Additionally, the hero gains new abilities as he levels up. The aim of the game is to destroy the opponent's Ancient, which is a large structure defended by the enemy team. While carrying out this objective, the team must protect their own Ancient and kill enemy players.

Dota-2 is a huge title within the esports industry. There have been over 800 tournaments completed and over $128 million awarded in prizes.

Counter-Strike: Global Offensive (CS:GO) ⊃ Value
                                                                      HiddenPath

CS:GO is the 4th game in the Counter-Strike series, released in 2012. It is a multiplayer first-person shooter video game that was developed by Hidden Path Entertainment and Valve Corporation. The game pits two teams against each other, aimed with the task of eliminating the enemy and completing

63

separate objectives. The objective is dependent on which of the six different game modes is played. The game modes are as follows:

- Competitive – This mode pits competitive players against each other in two teams of five.

- Casual & Death Match – These are less serious modes, primarily used for player practice.

- Arms Race – This mode is like the 'Gun Game', where players race to upgrade their guns via killing enemies.

- Demolition – This is similar to Arms Race, but players are required to plant and defuse the bomb.

- Weapons Course – This is an offline practice mode designed to help new players.

The Counter-Strike series have been prevalent within the esports space for some time now. CS:GO has had around 2800 tournaments played and $42 million in prize money issued.

Overwatch = Blizzard

Overwatch is a team based multiplayer online first-person shooter video game, developed and published by Blizzard Entertainment. It launched on the PC, PS4 and Xbox One in 2016.

Overwatch assigns players into two teams of six, with each player selecting from a roster of pre-defined 'Heroes'. Each of these characters have a unique style of play, which can be divided into four general categories:

1) Offence – Offence heroes have high mobility and the ability to deal large amounts of damage. To offset their strength, they have a low number of hit points

2) Defence – These characters excel at protecting specific locations and can provide means of support, such as sentry turrets and traps

3) Tank – These heroes have the most hit points as their role is to draw enemy fire away from their teammates to themselves. They have various means of protecting themselves with shield-like abilities.

4) Support – These utility heroes have abilities that
- enhance their own team or weaken the enemy team (using buffs and debuffs). They do not deal much damage, nor do they have much hit points.

Blizzard have developed and added new characters, maps and game modes post-release for free. The only additional costs to players are the in-game microtransactions. The developers have aimed to create a diverse cast of heroes that are balanced. Furthermore, they have tried to ensure that new players would be able to have fun, while skilled players would present each other with a challenge.

Upon release, Overwatch received universal acclaim from critics. The game has been praised for its accessibility, diverse appeal of hero characters and enjoyable gameplay. Overwatch has become a recognised esport, with Blizzard helping to fund and produce professional leagues and other tournament events. The developers have included and planned features for the game to support the competitive community. The game has enough variety in maps and characters, and strong support from Blizzard to maintain the game as a strong esport.

During the 2016 Blizzcon, Blizzard announced plans for their Overwatch league, using permanent teams in league placements like more traditional sports. Blizzard will help to organise potential team owners and aim to include more geographically-local teams to participate. This is with the aim of sparking more spectator and potential sponsor interest, built around supporting a local team.

Blizzard expect all players within the league to receive a salary. Furthermore, they anticipate that the Overwatch league will have a seven-figure payoff for the winning team at the end of the season.

Despite Overwatch only coming to the market in 2016, it has been successful on the esports scene. There have been around 500 tournaments to date, with over $5 million in prize money awarded.

FIFA Series = EA Sports

The FIFA series have been developed and published by EA Sports on an annual basis since 1993. The football game is notable for being the first to have an official license from FIFA (football governing body). Over the years, EA Sports have added many exclusively licensed leagues from around the world to the game, allowing the use of real leagues, clubs and player names.

Within the game there are several modes that can be leveraged by players. These include both offline and online modes. FIFA fans can play a head to head match with their friends, embark on a career mode with their favourite team or play online in three main modes. The three main online modes are:

1) Classic Online – In this mode, gamers compete against others online in a 'Season' system, using official teams. They play a set number of games per 'Season' and need to hit a target point threshold to be promoted to the next division.

2) Ultimate Team – This is EA Sports golden nugget, bringing in huge revenue for the publisher. In this mode, gamers build their 'Ultimate Team' through acquiring player cards in a variety of ways. They then play with their team against the computer or others online in a 'Season' system.

3) Pro Clubs – This is probably my favourite FIFA mode. In Pro Clubs, gamers create a 'Pro', setting his characteristics and qualities that determine his attributes within the game. Gamers can then join others in a team of up to eleven players and compete

in the 'Season' system to climb their way up to division one.

Additionally, within these three modes, players and teams (pro clubs) can play against other players and teams in arranged friendly matches.

FIFA is not a major esport title at this moment in time, despite its global dominance in the football video game market. For FIFA 17, there were only around 40 tournaments with $1.4 million in prize money. However, having watched this market for several years, I feel it is due exponential growth, particularly with EA Sports recently announcing their plans for the FIFA 18 eWorld Cup.

The video game series is the bestselling sports video game franchise in the world, and one of the bestselling video game franchises. FIFA 18 is the latest title in the series. In the future, we may see the disappearance of sequential FIFA series.

EA Sports chief executive Andrew Wilson recently revealed in an interview with Bloomberg that the FIFA series could become a subscription service, following a structure used by entities like Netflix and World of Warcraft.

By creating a year-round live service, gamers would simply purchase a recurring subscription that would give them access to FIFA. EA sports would then update, patch and improve the game year-round. Transfers and new features would be implemented on a rolling basis, with game modes being introduced by provision of a downloadable in-game update.

No more having to wait for the next release date to see your favourite football players in their new team.

This move feels natural as the gaming and digital world is moving from a disc world to one based on a subscription model. It would also reduce the dip in activity after several months from the release date, creating sustained engagement. From my experience, activity within the title is hugely seasonal, with the peak being around the release date.

Regardless of EA Sports' efforts to push the FIFA series into a 'top esport title' category, there are other things in this segment that need to be addressed before it can truly take off.

3.3 Game Publishers

The main activity of game publishers is to develop and commercialise video games for domestic use. When their video game acquires relevance in the field of esports, some publishers also participate in the organisation of events or establish some conditions for a competition using their video game.

In comparison to traditional sports, there are fewer content restrictions around major esports events. This is because game publishers are in the business of selling games, as opposed to selling media rights to competitions featuring their games. Despite this, within the esports market, the power lies with the game publishers. They can decide who, when and under what conditions can organise a competition around their product.

At this moment in time, esports is viewed by publishers primarily as a method for marketing their games. The more people that are seen to be playing the game within esports, the more people are likely to purchase the game or make micro-transactions within them. Additionally, the interest of traditional media presents new opportunities for game publishers to increase the exposure of the game title to a new audience. Ovum, a market research business, has forecasted global revenues generated from micro-transactions within PC games (such as LoL and Dota 2) will rise to a colossal $28.1 billion by 2019.

Game publishers evidently make more from game sales and micro-transactions than from fans directly watching the game, at this moment in time. As a result, the current balance of money indicates that it is more important for game publishers to nurture the grassroots to attract more gamers to play their game and make in-game purchases.

Game publishers are recognising the interest within esports, and so have sought to adopt the format of established sports tournaments to increase their game's appeal to television and brands. For example, EA sports have recently announced their Global Series on the road to the FIFA eWorld Cup 2018. Starting in November, this global ecosystem will feature more competitors and tournaments than before, where players will be able to participate in an array of online and live events to qualify for the Global Series play-offs. The Global Series will culminate with the first ever FIFA eWorld Cup 2018 Grand Final. By August 2018, the winner will be crowned the undisputed world FIFA champion.

Many publishers are now providing extensive statistics and data to the players and the community. In Dota-2 for example, every single player action from every single match can be downloaded by the esports community. The main use of these statistics is for analysis. Being able to access your own data, along with the ability to analyse and strategise, undoubtedly improves performance.

A professional team may have an analyst working for them, providing a dissection of matches and comprehensive analysis. However, the clear majority of the esports community are reliant on a few analyst providers and the tools built in to the game. There simply is not many effective, easy to use, tools to help utilise the data for the everyday gamer. I think game publishers need to take further steps to provide extensive tools to help teams and players analyse and engage with the data. In turn, this would be hugely beneficial for the grassroots esports community and therefore allows the future of esports to become more sustainable.

Valve have taken another approach to nurturing their gaming

community. They organise four Majors for Dota-2, which

culminate at The International. These majors are further

backed by open and regional qualifiers in multiple

geographies. Riot Games have also hosted the League of

Legends Championship Series across multiple territories,

including France, Germany, the UK and Belgium. This

investment in the grass roots of their respective games has

provided increased accessibility to competitions and

sustainability of the games as esports.

Valve have made significant additional steps in creating a

sustainable ecosystem for their games (Dota-2 & Counter

Strike). For example, players can spend money in CS:GO and

get special items. That money would go to valve with and a

sizeable portion (25%) put into an esports fund, which feeds

into tournament circuits. The community funds the

tournaments and Valve still make money in the process. The money spent would essentially feed back into the esports ecosystem, with the effect of increasing the player base.

Game publishers play a fundamental role within esports, as it is their product that is the focal point of any esport. Therefore, the esports industry is heavily reliant on game publishers. They will play a crucial role in the development of the nascent industry.

3.4 Esports Event Producers

Esports event producers make most of their revenue from sponsorship and advertising, sold around video streams associated with their content. The adoption of the structure of established sports within esport events further reflects the sense that esports is heading towards mainstream. The interest of traditional media provides the Event Producers with the additional opportunity to generate revenue from selling rights to broadcast the event.

There are gamers that play together online every night and often use these live events as an opportunity to meet in person. Event producers need to tie event experiences into the games that they love, in a fun way. There are plenty of ways of doing this, which inevitably would bring the community closer together. Furthermore, by providing digital tools and models (like you would see viewing an established traditional sport), the event is made easier to follow by fans.

Sometimes, the game publishers can play an active role in acting as competition operators. Often, it will be external operators that will produce esport events. The event producers will also play a crucial role in the development of esports. They play a fundamental role in providing a platform for gamers to engage with others on a competitive level.

I think it is important for esport event producers to consider catering for the grassroot gamers of the esports communities. Additionally, they should produce bespoke events that cater for the specific title they are providing competitions for. Presently, there are several operators that have diversified into providing competitions for several titles. This can be detrimental to their approach if they do not ensure that their competitions are tailored to the title's audience. Event producers should take the title and the target audience in mind when forming their competition.

Esports event producers will also play an imperative role in the future of esports. There are a few key established event producers in the space, such as MLG, ESL and DreamHack.

Major League Gaming (MLG) is a professional esports organisation founded in 2002, headquartered in New York. In 2016, MLG was acquired by Activision Blizzard. The organisation holds official video game competitions for games such as Call of Duty.

Electronic Sports League (ESL) is an esports company that organises video game competitions worldwide. ESL was founded in Germany back in 2000, and is one of the world's largest and oldest esports company that is still operational. They host pro leagues for a number of esports titles, including Overwatch, Counter Strike, Rocket League and Mortal Kombat, to name a few.

DreamHack is a Swedish based esports events and production company, founded in 1994. DreamHack usually hold event in Western Europe and North America, for titles such as League of Legends and Counter Strike.

3.5 Esports Teams

There is an ever-increasing number of teams and organisations within the esports landscape. Despite this, due to the infancy of the industry, there are teams and organisations here one day, and gone the next. This is demonstrated in the ranking of top 10 teams (www.esportsearnings.com) based on tournament prize money, player transfers and team statements published on the Internet. Several teams have become defunct, despite having earnt a significant amount of prize money. I have also included a few other noteworthy Esports Teams.

As you will see, many of these teams are global. This is particularly the case with multi-genre esport teams. They may be headquartered in one specific country, but their teams are often located in various countries around the world.

<u>Team Liquid (1)</u>

$17,684,421.65 overall team earnings (1091 Tournaments).

Team Liquid is a multi-regional, multi-genre professional esports organisation based in the Netherlands, founded in 2000. They originally started as a news site focussing on StarCraft. Then, following the release of StarCraft II in 2010, Team Liquid signed their first professional players.

In 2012, Team Liquid made their first venture into multi-genre management as they recruited a North American Dota-2 team. By 2015, Team Liquid then merged with Team Curse, bringing in League of Legends, Street Fighter and Super Smash Bros teams. They now have teams in a variety of other genres, including Overwatch, Halo, Counter Strike and Heroes of the Storm.

Team Liquid's Dota-2 squad won the International 2017, winning $11 million in prize money from a tournament that has had the largest prize pool for a tournament in esports history. Their partners include HTC, Monster Energy, Twitch and Discord.

Evil Geniuses (2)

$16,513,384.93 overall team earnings (671 Tournaments)

Evil Geniuses are an esports organisation based in the United States and founded in 1999. Originally, they were founded as a Counter-Strike team but now they have many divisions, fielding players in various fighting games, as well as other hugely popular games such as Dota-2, LoL, Halo and Call of Duty, to name a few.

Evil Geniuses Dota-2 division won the International 2015, receiving the largest prize reward in esports history at the time ($6.6 million). The organisation has some big partners, which include Monster Energy, Xfinity, SanDisk, AMD and Twitch.

Newbee (3)

$11,892,337.79 overall team earnings (105 Tournaments)

Newbee is a Chinese based esports organisation founded in 2014. Newbee fields players in Dota-2, Hearthstone and League of Legends. Their Dota-2 squad won the 2014 International, receiving a prize of over $5 million.

LGD Gaming (4)

$10,048,136.10 overall team earnings (108 Tournaments)

LGD Gaming are an esports organisation also based in China, founded in 2009. They have teams competing in Dota-2 and

League of Legends tournaments. Their Dota-2 team has reached the International for five years consecutively. They came 3rd in 2012 ($150,000 prize), 5th-6th in 2014 ($650,000 prize) and 3rd in 2015 ($2.2 million prize).

Wings Gaming (5)

$9,718,065.87 overall team earnings (22 Tournaments)

Wings Gaming is a defunct Chinese Dota-2 esports team, founded in 2014 and folded in 2017. They were best known for winning over $9 million at the International 2016. They were also nominated as the esports team of the year at The Game Awards 2016.

In 2017, all five of the playing members left the team and played under the banner of Team Random at a Dota-2 Major. Following a bottom placed finish, the team disbanded, with many of the players taking a break from professional Dota-2.

SK Telecom T1 (6)

$8,478,931.94 overall team earnings (211 Tournaments)

This team is run by the South Korean telecommunications company, SK Telecom. SK Telecom T1 was founded in 2002, primarily competing in League of Legends competitions. The team is part of SK Sports, which includes South Korean baseball, football and basketball teams. They have been sponsored by a number of brands, such as the apparel company New Balance.

Fnatic (7)

$8,397,014.42 overall team earnings (669 Tournaments)

Fnatic is a professional esports organisation that was founded in 2004. The organisation is headquartered in London, United Kingdom, but fields players from around the world in a variety of games. The games that Fnatic compete in include Counter-strike, Rocket League, Call of Duty, League of Legends and Dota-2

Fnatic are renowned for winning the first ever League of Legends World Championship in 2011. Furthermore, the organisation have one of the best Counter-strike teams of all time, having won three CS:GO Majors and many other tournaments with the other titles in the series.

Fnatic's partners include AMD, Fnatic Gear, GG.bet, NewZoo and Twitch TV.

Virtus.pro (8)

$7,721,404.04 overall team earnings (323 Tournaments)

Virtus Pro are an esports organisation that has competing teams in Counter-strike, Dota-2, World of Tanks, League of

Legends, to name a few. They are based in Russia and were founded in 2003. In 2015, the organisation received an investment of over $100 million from Alisher Usmanov's USM Holdings. Usmanov also is a key shareholder in Arsenal FC, and is reportedly worth $15.1 billion.

Invictus Gaming (9)

$7,082,799.40 overall team earnings (343 Tournaments)

Invictus Gaming is another multi-game esports organisation based in China and founded in 2011. They are primarily known for their Dota-2, League of Legends and StarCraft II teams, but also field teams in a number of other games.

Invictus Gaming's Dota-2 team won the International in 2012, winning $1 million in prize money.

Vici Gaming (10)

$6,657,922.62 overall team earnings (184 Tournaments)

This Chinese based professional esports organisation was founded in 2012. Vici Gaming are also a multi-game esports organisation, fielding teams in Dota-2, League of Legends, StarCraft II, FIFA and Counter-strike.

The Dota-2 division has performed well in many competitions, most notably finishing runner up at the International 2014 after losing to Newbee. Vici Gaming also have many partners, including the likes of HTC.

Cloud9 (13)

$5,792,795.32 overall team earnings (487 tournaments)

Cloud9 are an American multi-game esports organisation, fielding teams in a large number of games. They were founded in 2012, focussing initially on League of Legends. Following the success of the LoL team in North America, the team expanded to cover a range of other games including Call of Duty, Dota-2, Hearthstone, Super Smash Bros, Rocket League and Overwatch.

SK Gaming (18)

$4,729,165.51 overall team earnings (508 tournaments)

SK Gaming is an esports organisation based in Germany, founded in 1997 by a small group of Quake players. SK

Gaming primarily focus on Counter-strike, Hearthstone and Vainglory (mobile esports title).

Their Counter-strike team is based in Brazil and won the ESL One Cologne 2016 Major, defeating some of the top ten teams in the process. The prize for winning that major was $500,000.

SK gaming have performed exceptionally well over the years in various tournaments. Sponsors of SK Gaming include Toshiba, VISA, Intel, Kingston Technology and Mountain Dew.

OpTic Gaming (19)

$4,640,849.12 overall team earnings (204 tournaments)

OpTic Gaming, also known as the Green Wall, are a professional esports organisation based in America. They were founded in 2006 and boast teams in Call of Duty, Halo, Counter-strike, Gears of War and Dota-2. The organisation holds many rivalries, most notably eClassico with Team EnVyUs (another American based esports organisation)

The organisation won the X Games two years consecutively where they competed in Call of duty and Counter-strike competitions (2014 and 2015). OpTic Gaming won the best esports team of the year at The Game Awards 2015. In 2017, they clinched their first Call of Duty World Championship.

G2 Esports (26)

$2,492,781.23 overall team earnings (216 tournaments)

G2 Esports, also known as Gamers2, is a Spanish esports organisation that launched in 2014 and has teams in League of Legends, Counter-strike, Hearthstone, Rocket league and FIFA 18 to name a few.

G2 has numerous partners which include Vodafone, Paysafecard and Kingston HyperX.

Team Dignitas (30)

$2,432,122.12 overall team earnings (445 tournaments)

Team Dignitas is a UK based international esports organisation, founded around 2004, initially for Battlefield but then expanded into a wider range of games. Team

Dignitas has four main divisions right now; Counter-strike, League of Legends, Heroes of the Storm and Smite. Their League of Legends team currently competes in the North American League of Legends Championship Series.

In 2016, a professional basketball team, Philadelphia 76ers, acquired the organisation. Team Dignitas' partners include Alienware, Buffalo Wild Wings, Mountain Dew and HyperX.

3.6 Esports Players

Professional esports players may train for several hours a day to ensure they have extremely fast reflexes and reactions. In some esports titles, players may be required to make more than 300 actions per minute, so they need to be able to multi-task well. Furthermore, if there is an update, the gamers need to make sure that they have mastered any changes that have taken place.

The best players are often on the steepest learning curves. Often these star gamers have been thrust into a limelight for which neither they, nor the industry, were fully prepared. No other sport, except maybe Golf, have dynamics whereby regular players can use the same characters and play on the same field as the stars. Furthermore, thanks to streaming platforms like Twitch, fans can watch their favourite esport players practice online and engage with them.

Although esport professional players have some of the least power compared to the key players, they are central to the welfare of the industry. Without the players, esports would not be able to have grown to the height it has. It is obvious that if there are not popularity among players for a game, often it would not be a successful esports title.

3.7 Esports Viewers

Esports viewers are another key component of the esports industry. Without the 385 million strong esports fan base, the industry would not be growing at the rate it is. The viewers and the players are the heart of esports.

The young, male and decision-making profile of this audience is what is enabling the market to become so lucrative and appealing for advertisers and brands. Esports needs revenue to be able to provide viewers with what they enjoy so much!

It is the size and profile of these viewers that are driving huge investment into the industry. All other key players within esports must realise that this is the case and ensure that the viewers are looked after. They need to be listened to and kept engaged. If a game loses its viewer base for competitions, it will begin to decline within esports.

3.8 Esports Competitions

When esports first started, the money was not there. Tournaments were hosted inside lobbies of hotels and the pay-out was just a couple thousand dollars. However, as the industry has grown, the number of tournaments have proliferated, and the prize money has increased considerably.

Esports competitions have many different formats, with various subtypes. These variables can include:

- Match Types – Best out of one, two or three games

- Group Stages – Round robin, double round robin or swiss seeding.

- Knockout Stages – Single or double elimination bracket.

Globally, ESL, Blizzard, Riot Games and MLG are the organisers that have hosted the most tournaments in 2016. The total prize money awarded in 2016, in events with a prize pool of above $5000, was $93.3 million. That is a 52.9% increase from 2015, where $61 million was the total prize money awarded.

Below are some of the major esports competitions. There are many other competitions that have also been established and many others that are on the horizon. One thing is for certain; these competitions play a key role in providing gamers and teams with the opportunity to compete at a professional level, providing financial incentives at the same time.

The International (Dota-2)

The International is an annual Dota-2 esports championship tournament, hosted by Valve Corporation. The first championship tournament took place in Germany back in 2011, with a total prize pool of $1.6 million.

The prize pool has increased over the years up to the recent 2017 International, with a prize pool of $24 million. The 2017 championship has been awarded the biggest prize pool in esports history, breaking the record set by the previous year's tournament.

Intel Extreme Masters

The IEM is the longest running tournament in esports. It has been put on by Electronic Sports League (ESL) and Intel since 2006. The location of the tournament changes city every year. It has been held in Dubai, Los Angeles, Hanover and many other cities. The 2016 IEM was held in Poland and had around 115,000 attendees.

The Intel Extreme Masters esports tournaments cover a host of games, including StarCraft II, Counter Strike: Global Offensive and League of Legends to name a few.

Riot Games Franchised Leagues

Riot Games have introduced a franchised league in North America starting in 2018, where permanent League of Legend teams are in the line-up. A player's association will be set up and a minimum salary of $75,000 per individual player will be implemented. The teams will have to pay a $10 million fee, demonstrating the lucrativeness of this league.

The structure of the league will have a revenue sharing model, whereby league based revenues (media rights) and league driven revenues (sponsorship and merchandise sales) would be shared. Moreover, a media right deal with BAMTech (subsidiary of the Walt Disney Company) for $300 million has been confirmed.

League of Legends World Championship

The League of Legends World Championship is the annual professional world championship, hosted by Riot Games. It is the finale for each season, where teams compete for the champion title along with a Summoner's Cup and $1 million prize. In 2016, the finals were watched by 43 million people, with 396 million total cumulative daily unique impressions.

Furthermore, Riot Games allowed consumer contribution to the competition, driving the prize pool to more than $5 million.

The LoL World Championship has gained tremendous success and popularity, making it among the world's most prestigious and watched tournaments, surpassing many sports tournaments.

The Evolution Championship Series

This annual sports event focuses exclusively on fighting games. The tournament is an open tournament that uses the double elimination format, whereby participants become ineligible to win the tournament if they have lost two games. The first Evolution tournament took place in 1996, where players competed in the Super Street Fighter II Turbo and

Street Fighter Alpha 2 games. Every successive tournament since its conception has seen an increase in attendees.

Evo 2017 took place at the Mandala Bay resort featuring a host of fighting games, including Street Fighter V, Tekken 7 and Ultimate Marvel v Capcom 3 to name a few.

3.9 Brands in Esports: Case Studies & Tips

As alluded to earlier, according to Nielsen, there have been over 600 esports sponsorship since 2016. Majority of these coming from the IT/computer space. Nielsen's Fan Report also found that 50-60% of respondents have favourable responses towards brand involvement in esports events and streams. Only 10% provided negative responses to brand activity. Improving the favourable perceptions of brand involvement from fans is fundamental to making esports an even more attractive industry. This can be achieved through education of the importance of brand involvement and also by deploying the right strategy in activation of sponsorship.

Nielsen indicates that more than 360 IT/computer sponsorships have been secured, followed by 100+ deals in retail, 60+ online services, 50+ non-alcoholic drinks and 40+ online media. So far, the top categories that have entered the esports space include: energy drinks, fast food, headsets, PC technology, PC hardware, gaming software, esports news and gaming chairs. Other categories include the automotive industry and the lending market.

There are different forms of sponsorship within esports. Brands can choose to associate with broadcast platforms, teams, players and events. With the way that esports operates currently, sometimes it makes more sense to sponsor players than teams. There is instability within the landscape, we see professionals switching teams all the time, and often their name carries more weight than the team name. As stability among teams, rosters and generally within esports increases, the number of brands sponsoring entities within the space will correlatively increase.

Sponsoring content is a way for brands to get past ad-blocking, but it must be done right. Brands must want to add value to the users and audience, not frustrate them. The brand needs to be taken and tied in with the player, team or event. The sponsorship needs to support the esports movement and be transparent. If you frustrate the viewers by being too invasive, it could affect your bottom line.

Brands looking to enter the space need to consider an altruistic, authentic and long-term strategy if they want success. Millennials are cause-driven individuals, and esports is a cause now. It is a niche market that is trying to establish itself mainstream and so brands that aim to lead the charge in driving the industry forward will be most successful. It is not as simple as having your brand logo placed on merchandise, but about improving the space. Questions you should ask when activating in the esports space are; Whether your strategy will authenticate esports into mainstream culture?

Are you helping teams become more competitive? Are you providing opportunities for those within the esports space?

In March 2017, Magid Advisors surveyed 1000 consumers aged 16 – 45 in conjunction with the esports Ad Bureau. More than half the respondents said they watched a live esports event at least once a week, while 72% of these avid fans said they want advertisers to add value for the entire esports community. Fans also seem to not object to brand integration, if they make sense. They also favour advertisers providing product discounts to event attendees and the viewing audience.

Below are a few case studies of brands that have put money into esports in the hopes of reaching the elusive demographics that have become increasingly hard to reach via traditional advertising:

Coca Cola

Coke's approach has been to utilize fan passion for esports. This includes some old-fashioned techniques, such as handing out 'cheer boards' at events which allow fans to scribble messages on them. Additionally, Coke also hosts viewing parties of big events at cinemas for those that cannot make it. For the 2016 League of Legends World Championship, Coke provided viewings for more than 200 movie screens across the US.

Coca Cola have a partnership with Riot Games, activating at the LoL tournaments across the US. They offer additional value to the fans as well as supplying their drinks. They have gone further and partnered with EA Sports FIFA to create a minor-league tournament for amateur players to compete in their first gaming competition. It is called the FIFA eCOPA Coca Cola and targeted college-aged gamers. Winners receive a cash scholarship along with entry to a professional esports event – EA Sports FIFA 17 Ultimate Team Regional Finals.

Gillette

Gillette activated at the Intel Extreme Masters tournament in Poland. They offered free grooming services to all competitors, as well as providing fans and players with a chance to customize their own 3D printed razor.

Bud Light

Bud Light had a difficult time when initially entering the space. Gamers tend to be sceptical of outsiders, particularly big brands. Bud Light activated by creating a group of 'Bud Light All-Stars', consisting of esports competitors. The final selections for the all-stars were chosen by fans from a group of players nominated by the brand.

Bud Light were criticized and accused of actually searching for brand ambassadors as opposed to actually finding the best. Dotesports.com even went as far as saying the players nominated were not good enough.

Despite the criticism, Bud Light were resilient and pressed on. As they started creating content featuring the all-stars, the pessimism began to evaporate. They have stated that they have been more than happy with the results and planned to continue the program in 2017.

Totinos (Pizza)

Totinos are brands of frozen pizza products. They activated at the Intel Extreme Masters in Oakland by providing ample samples to the masses. Additionally, they challenged gamers to remain on the red couches, that acted as moving (spinning devices), while trying to play a video game.

Comcast Xfinity

Comcast Xfinity is a high-speed internet provider that also activated in Oakland. The activation was operated by Comcast employees who are avid gamers themselves. They were ideal to lead the strategy as they knew the products and understood how to use the products for gaming purposes. This meant that the employees were able to converse about the actual event and have genuine conversations with fans, which no doubt provided authenticity.

Comcast craftily have gone for two partnerships. One is with ESL and the other is with the gaming team Evil Geniuses. This structure enables the brand to capture the excitement that fans have over their favourite team, as well as providing the brand with a more traditional play to run advertising and branding.

Going further, Evil Geniuses are a top team that operates out of two large Comcast markets – the Bay Area and Chicago. As part of the agreement, Comcast Xfinity's branding features on the Evil Geniuses jerseys. In return, the brand have sponsored training facilities and provided them with a premium Internet service, among other things.

Comcast's strategy with Evil Geniuses is one of natural integration, so when the players speak about the brands or products, it is much more authentic.

<u>Other Sponsors:</u>

Other brands that have had a big impact on esports and the gaming community in general include:

- IGN
- Twitch
- Gamestop
- YouTube
- Google
- Microsoft & Sony
- Doritos
- Redbull
- Nerdist
- Nissan
- Audi

You only need to look at how traditional sports have integrated sponsors for direction. Good sponsorship agreements work where the sponsor appears to be part of the show. This is what advertisers should look for – the goal of being treated as part of the production you are putting on. This is when you will see positive results from the sponsorship. To do this, brands need to look after the core fans by building and engaging with them. By being part of the cause with good intentions of wanting to further the player, the team or an event, you will become part of the movement.

Brands need to be careful to not upset the balance of the programme by activating in a way that does not makes sense. Additionally, it is critical that the viewers and fans are treated like people, as opposed to numbers or a revenue source.

3.10 Esports Associations

There have been many Esport associations formed over the years, all with a synergetic ambition to drive the esports industry forward.

The International esports Federation (IeSF) is probably the most developed governing body, growing from 9 eSport associations in 2008 to 47-member nations currently. It aims to promote esports and its players, and to standardise the industry.

Additionally, the World Esport Association (WESA) was founded in 2016 by the esports veterans, ESL, along with many esport teams. Founding members include big names such as Fnatic, Ninjas in Pyjamas and G2 Esports. It is another organisation that aims to set standards, help bring consistency and regulation to competitions, and organise the broader world of esports. WESA aims professionalise the industry through regulations, player representation and revenue shares for teams. It currently regulates the Counter

Strike ESL Pro League for now, but hopes to add more leagues and teams in the future.

The British Esports Association (BEA) is the national body for esports in the UK. It has been designed to provide support and promote grass roots esports in Britain. In doing so, the BEA aims to provide esports with credibility as an activity by focussing on the positive benefits when done in moderation.

The Esports Integrity Coalition (ESIC) was formed in 2015. It is another association that hopes to be the recognised body taking responsibility for disruption, prevention, investigation and prosecution of all forms of cheating.

3.11 Esport Media Broadcasters

- Twitch

- Youtube

- Facebook

- Traditional Media Outlets – ESPN & Turner

Twitch TV and YouTube are the most dominant esport media broadcasters presently, and are currently fighting for market share. At this moment in time, Twitch appears to be the market leader, with Youtube generating competition. The direct attempt from Youtube to dethrone Twitch came in 2015, when they provided the ability for users to broadcast live via YouTube Gaming. Interestingly, Twitch allows for gamers to take their highlights to YouTube, and YouTube provides a notification to the gaming audience when the creator is live on Twitch. So, a fan can be watching their favourite player's content on YouTube and then head over to Twitch when the notification pops up that the player is live.

Online platforms, such as Twitch, provide viewers with statistics and the ability to switch between the video feeds of different players. YouTube's advantage is that it has a far wider social community for esport fans to share content with. The platform attracts avid and casual gaming consumers on a large global scale. It is crucial that an esports content creator use both platforms to grow the brand and audience.

Facebook, armed with 1.6 billion users, have made moves to get into the game. They partnered with live video content providers, including Activision Blizzard Media Networks, to show live content via MLG.tv's Facebook page. MLG.tv also provide viewers with a feed of match statistics, live leaderboards and insights based on the competition they are watching.

Other esport video platforms include Azubu, Hitbox, uStream and StreamMe. These are similar but much smaller than Twitch and YouTube.

Conventional TV have tried to get involved by acquiring esport content producers and by creating its own content. In the US, ESPN began by streaming games on their website. They then expanded to provide blocks of esports broadcasting on their ESPN2 and ESPNU TV Channels. Recently, European broadcaster Sky launched the Ginx.TV channel to air esports competitions.

Another potential route to broadcasting esports is in investing vertically. Turner Broadcasting and WME-IMG invested vertically by creating the Eleague around Counter Strike. Coverage for the league is distributed on the TBS TV channel and on Twitch.

There are a few improvements that can be made to esports coverage. Presently, coverage has been confined to commentary of player versus player, with little context and broader narrative. It is this contextual storytelling that will allow esports broadcasting to soar to untold heights. There needs to be more pre- and post-game analysis along with more exposure in relation to individual player's stories.

Content around analysis and side stories that creates additional storylines around tournaments would provide more engaging content for the audience. Furthermore, it provides the audience with emotional context to the players, teams and the game, making matches more meaningful.

3.12 Comparison with Traditional Sports

The significant audience and commercial cross over with traditional sports is worth evaluating. In this section, I will discuss the key differences and similarities between traditional sports and esports.

Classification as a Sport

Labelling video games as sports is a controversial point of debate. Much like professional athletes, gamers spend large amounts of time developing new skills that will help them compete in their games. Often the core rules of the game do not change, but the dynamics change as new characters and environments are added. Players constantly go through strategies to combat the different scenarios that they may encounter in a game. Gamers also need to have very fast reaction times and the capability to keep up with the pace of the action.

Esports can be considered a "real sport" by definition, much in the same way as chess or poker can be. There are many parallels between traditional athletic sports and esports. However, the virtual environment and lack of physical activity call into question whether we can truly define esports as "real sports" rather than a "mind sport". Like poker and chess, esports are mind-based sports with limited physical activity. Some definitions use words like 'usually' and 'or' when talking about the physical activity involved. This further makes the case for the fact that sports need not always be physical athletic activity. The physical exertion and outdoor playing areas are not required by all traditional or non-traditional 'sports'

According to the US Federal Government, esport players are considered professional athletes. In 2013, a Canadian League of Legends became the first pro gamer to receive a United

States P-1A visa, a category designated for 'Internationally Recognised Athletes' allowing a stay of up to 5 years. In 2016, the French Government started working on a project to regulate and recognise esports. Recently, they passed legislation which regulates professional esport player contracts within their country.

Although many argue that popularity of esports should justify competitive gaming as a sport, I believe it is the careful planning, precise timing and skilful execution that should support the activity's classification as a sport.

Esports Leagues Compared with Traditional Sport Leagues

Esport leagues are volatile places where commercially viable teams are here one day and gone the next – like the early big four North American leagues.

Take the NBA as an example. It was formed in 1949 when the Basketball Association of America and the National Basketball League merged, with sixteen teams. By 1955, only eight of these teams were still around. Original NFL franchises also came and went in the 1920s as the league found its footing. NHL also barely survived its first year as one of its four teams (Montreal Wanderers) disbanded after their arena burned down.

So, what gave the leagues stability and helped them grow? A host of changes. Changes that fuelled profitability, aligned the owners' interest and helped them run their business in a predictable manner, on the field and on the balance sheet. The stability of franchises, revenue sharing agreements, player centric features and other elements from traditional sports can be used to create a more predictable ecosystem for game publishers, owners, players, sponsors and other esports industry participants.

Traditional sports can take a page out of esports book as well. They can look to improve on interactivity and live streaming of events.

Other Key Differences & Similarities

When you see someone do something good in a video game, you can literally go and do that thing. Traditional sports, you can see someone do something on the field, but you would need two teams of players, a field and so on. Esports is more accessible for the public and there is a much thinner barrier between the player and the viewer.

Additionally, esports tend to have a sequel like nature, with games rules and dynamics changing from game to game. On the other hand, in traditional sports, there are no football 2 or basketball 2. This characteristic causes instability and a lack of longevity within esports. Despite this, often games keep the core rules the same. I can see publishers dropping the numbers to sequels in the future.

3.13 Esports Betting

Simply put, esports betting is gambling on the outcome of an esports event. The bettors can use skins (virtual currency) as well as bet with real money. Esports, although in its infancy, has matured over the years to the point that it is now on par with some of the leading major sports in terms of viewership, following and interest.

Many of the world's leading betting operators have recognised the opportunity and potential growth within esports and consequently, for some time now, offer esports betting options alongside their traditional products. Esports betting operators include Betway, Ladbrokes, William Hill, Sky Bet, Paddy Power, Mr Green and Pinnacle. They take bets on numerous esports matches and the volume of bets placed already exceed that of golf, tennis and rugby.

Betting operators see esports as a huge 'blue ocean' opportunity. As seen from sports betting, the gambling industry is a far bigger business than media rights, sponsorships and consumer revenues put together. Take NFL for example, generating over $13 billion in 2016. Betting and fantasy leagues around the NFL games are supposed to have generated north of $50 billion.

The global gambling industry has got to the point that it needs to appeal to a new type of customer. It is primarily the ability to tap into the millennial market that is so enticing to the operators. This target market is one which has always been of great interest to gambling operators around the world. A market which is more demanding, inquisitive and digitally savvy. Esports betting is and will be bigger than the esports industry itself.

Particularly when esport tournaments are fast paced events, competitive and have a live crowd creating atmosphere – comparable to traditional sport events like a football match.

Market research firm Eilers & Krejcik Gaming had projected that the unregulated esports betting market would generate the amount of $7.4 billion in betting turnover by the end of 2016. When combined with turnover from regulated betting operations, overall bets probably exceed $8 billion last year. Furthermore, Eilers project fans will spend around $23 billion on esports betting by 2020, with operators generating more than $1.8 billion in revenue from this betting pool.

Although esports betting targets primarily males between the ages of 18 and 25, minors can also easily bet on the outcome of matches. The esports betting industry needs regulation for a safe and well-functioning environment to be developed. Effective regulation should enforce the exclusion of those under the eligible age.

Several regulators have announced their stance on esports betting, with specific mention of skin betting. The Isle of Man has recently allowed the licensed provision of skin betting options. On the other hand, the Norwegian Gaming Authority have declared that they consider skin betting a gambling activity. With online gambling operations being conducted by a state-run monopoly, Norway have issued a warning stating that any operator offering this service will face a penalty.

The UK Gambling Commission have also discussed skin betting, publishing a paper on esports in the process. They warned parents about the risks skin betting poses to their underaged children and assured action against unauthorized websites that provide this type of offering.

Chapter 4: Previous Research in Esports

There are two key recent reports published that are worth analysing; The Nielsen Report (The Esports Playbook: maximising investment through understanding the fans) and the NewZoo Report (The Global Esports Market Report. Both have been published in 2017, but The Nielsen Report focusses primarily on the fans, whereas the NewZoo report focusses on the market.

In this chapter, I will summarise the key findings from both reports, while also providing an evaluation and analysis.

4.1 The Nielsen Report

In this section, I will summarise the key findings from the report published on 3rd October 2017. Nielsen Market Intelligence aimed to provide an in-depth study into esport fans, in the hope that it would impact the growth and brand investment into the space. The study primarily targeted fans in the US, UK, France and Germany, with the goal of providing an insight into the complex picture of this audience. It is apparent that the esports fan base is undoubtedly growing, but there are noteworthy differences across markets, game genres and individual titles that should be considered when discussing esports.

Audience Snapshot

In comparison with traditional sports, Nielsen found that the esports audience are younger, with an average age of 26 (traditional sports fans average age - 28). Furthermore, there is a greater proportion of males within the esports audience (71% for esports as opposed to 61% for broader traditional sports).

The younger, male profile of the esports audience provides the industry with the unique ability to tap into this increasingly elusive demographic. This ability is one that brands are finding extremely appealing.

Nielsen also identified that 61% of esports fans live in households with 3+ people. From this, it can be inferred that the fans are part of and make purchasing decisions for the household. This further reaffirms the attractiveness of brands entering the esports space.

The report also suggested that only 17% of both esports' fans leisure time and money is spent on gaming. This debunks the stereotype that all gamers spend most of their time and money playing video games. Going further, the report highlights that, on average, an esports fan spends approximately:

- 4 hours watching TV per week
- 8 hours playing video games per week
- 4.5 hours watching internet videos
- 5.6 hours social networking
- 6.5 hours surfing the internet.

From these figures, it appears the average esports fan spends nearly double the time playing video games than watching TV on a TV screen. The small proportion of their time watching

TV further cements the fact that it is no longer as effective to use traditional forms of marketing to target this elusive audience.

In terms of interaction, the young esports audience tend to use a variety of social media channels:

- Facebook – 57%

- Twitter – 42%

- Instagram – 36%

- Snapchat – 34%

- Reddit – 22%

Geographical Segments

Further analysis has provided various points of difference among fans in the US, UK, France and Germany. Understanding these segments and differences are essential as a singular approach will not reach all the fans effectively.

Firstly, it is important to understand the popularity of platforms in these regions. The report identifies the most popular platforms esports fans play games on. The Xbox One is just about as popular in both the UK and US markets, whereas esports fans are less likely to game on the Xbox One in Germany and France. It is also worth noting that British fans are least likely to play games on the computer compared to the other regions. In my opinion, I think this is because of the stigma still attached to gaming on computers in the UK.

Platforms/Location	US	UK	Germany	France
Xbox One	35%	32%	12%	19%
PS4	34%	35%	32%	34%
Computer	50%	39%	51%	54%

Secondly, in terms of when fans started following esports, it seems that UK is the least established compared to the other three major Western markets. Germany appears to be the most established market with 19% of fans having followed esports for more than 4+ years.

When Started Following Esports	US	UK	Germany	France
Within last year	29%	34%	30%	34%
1-3 years ago	55%	55%	51%	52%
4+ years ago	16%	11%	19%	14%

Additionally, the report indicates that there are three major influences in becoming esport fans:

1) Friends or family members
2) Youtuber, vlogger, online personality, entertainer...
3) Interest in a game that lead to esports

All three of these have a huge impact across the four western markets in influencing fans to follow esports. According to the report, French esport fans are more likely to have been drawn to esports through friends and family. Furthermore, French and German fans are more likely to have been engaged via the influence of online personalities.

Lastly, in relation to the active following of esports personalities and teams – the report indicates that French fans are more likely to follow esports online personalities, while US gamers are more likely to actively follow specific pro gamers and/or teams. The UK has the lowest active following of online personalities and pro teams compared to the other markets.

4.2 NewZoo Report

The 2017 Global Esports Market Report provides an in-depth look at the esports economy and a realistic estimate of its future potential in terms of trends, viewers, participants and revenue streams. This 119-page report was published on 14th February 2017.

The report forecast that the esports economy will grow to around $696 million this year. That is a 41.3% increase from 2016.

This year, brands are expected to spend $516 million, which is broken down into advertising ($155m), sponsorship ($266m) and media rights ($95m). Consumer spending on tickets and merchandise this year will amount to $64 million. Additionally, another $116 million is invested by game publishers into the esports industry through partnership deals. NewZoo predict that brand investment is expected to double by 2020, pushing the total market to $1.5 billion.

The report states that the global esports audience will reach 385 million this year. This global audience is made up of 191 million esports enthusiasts and a further 194 million occasional viewers. The number esports enthusiasts is expected to grow by 50% by 2020, totalling 286 million.

In the report, NewZoo examine the total revenue per esports fan to identify how well the industry is monetised. The report expects that the average revenue per fan this year will amount to $3.64. This is still significantly lower than traditional sports such as basketball and NFL. However, as the industry matures and incorporates an increasing number of local events, leagues and media right deals, the average revenue per fan is anticipated to grow to $5.20 by 2020.

In terms of the different regions, NewZoo highlights that North America is the largest esports market. North America has revenues of $257 million in 2017 and will more than double to reach $607 million by 2020. Most of this revenue comes from sponsorships, totalling $113 million in 2017. The reason for North America leading the boom could be partly due to the teams welcoming a lot of new non-endemic sponsorships. Furthermore, the region hosts some of the world's largest leagues and tournaments that generate a high amount of sponsorship money. The esport fans in this region also generate twice as much revenue per year than any other region ($10.36 per fan per year). This highlights the lead that North America has taken.

4.3 Business Insiders Report

Robert Elder, Research Analyst for 'Business Insiders'
Intelligence - compiled a comprehensive report on the esports
ecosystem that dissects the growing market for competitive
gaming.

Here are the key findings from the report:

- Esports is a still nascent industry filled with significant
  commercial opportunity.
- There are a variety of revenue streams that companies can
  tap into.
- The market is presently undervalued and has significant
  room to grow.
- The dynamism of this market distinguishes it from
  traditional sports.

- The audience is high-value and global, and its numbers are rising.

- Brands can prosper in esports by following the appropriate game plan.

- Game publishers approach their Esport ecosystems in different ways.

- Successful esport games are comprised of the same basic ingredients.

- Digital streaming platforms are spearheading the popularity of esports.

- Legacy media are investing into esports, and seeing encouraging results.

- Traditional sports franchises have a clear opportunity to seize in esports.

- Virtual and augmented reality firms also stand to benefit from esports.

Chapter 5: Opportunities & Challenges in Esports

5.1 Opportunities in Esports

The current growth rate and projections for the esports industry indicate that there are, and will be, significant opportunities within the landscape. This comes in the form of career opportunities, entertainment and a significant positive impact on the economy, on a global and regional scale.

The exciting thing about esports is how it converges various established industries. As the space grows and the potential is realised, these established industries will have more involvement within the space. I can see purpose built esports stadiums being built to accommodate the needs of the market. I can see huge domestic and international competitions with large communities supporting them. The trajectory of esports indicates that ample opportunity will arise within a whole host of industries. This includes the opportunity to build something within the esports industry, esports betting and fantasy sites.

If you compare the opportunities available to the wider public around twenty years ago to presently, you will see that there are significant opportunities now available that previously were not. This can be contributable to a number of factors, such as globalisation and improved technology. Esports is a niche market that is relatively new, and hence there will undoubtedly be significant opportunities for those in the space. Many of the opportunities will be innovative and new, developed as a result of the growth of the industry.

5.2 Careers in Esports

The esports industry is in its infancy and has a lot of space to grow. Naturally, because of this growth, opportunities and careers will develop as various established industries converge. Furthermore, as more endemic and non-endemic organisations recognise the industry's potential, I believe that new positions in relations to esports would be formed.

The usual skills plus an excellent esports acumen would be fruitful in pursuit of any role within the industry. Moreover, whatever path you decide to embark on, it would be hugely beneficial to stay relevant, know your sector and have an appreciation of gaming. Understanding the different disciplines within esports is critical to being successful within esports.

If you are pursuing a career in esports, it is fundamental to network. Utilise LinkedIn to build your network and find people who you wish to work with. Following from this, do not be afraid to offer your time or ask for what you want. Even if you have experience and think your talented, it is your responsibility to go out there and tell people what you can do, why you can do it, why you have been doing it and what you will be able to do in the future.

With the age of the industry, entrepreneurial spirit with the motivation to get involved and create something will go a long way. By embarking on a career in esports, showing dedication and figuring out ways to do things when money is not available can be hugely appealing to big corporations. Additionally, it would be handy to be able to utilise various conventional tools used in business, such as the Microsoft packages. Using PowerPoint and Excel, you can put together your plan in an effective way, showing preparation and thought.

You may have to volunteer and pay your dues, but you must go out and get what you want by selling yourself. Be energetic and an extrovert. The successful people within esports come from a place of passion. Be busy and create value. Do not be discouraged if you are not seeing results as it takes time and it is the act of doing that is critical to your long-term goals.

In this section I will outline the opportunities and careers that are available in esports now or potentially in the future. In terms of salary for many of these roles, the rates will vary according to regions.

Pro Gamers/Players

The new breed of esports athletes, with fine motor skills, focus, sharp reflexes and math skills, are attracting high-profile sponsorships. With tournament viewership in the multimillions, large prize pools and active betting frameworks, esports is truly blowing up. There is an growing shift to increased pro gamer profitability within the industry.

Players often start off in amateur or grassroots tournaments, reaching higher rankings within a game. This then can catch the attention of bigger teams and a player can be signed by the team to compete in different tournaments for prize money. The beauty of pro gamers within esports is the fine line between players and fans. Fans are often fellow gamers and due to the nature of the industry, any fan can become a pro, given the right opportunity and commitment.

Players will need to get along with their teammates, and work with a variety of disciplines, including managers, coaches and analysts. Furthermore, pro gamers may be required to travel all over the world to take part in competitions.

Another aspect to the role of a pro gamer entails participating in sponsor or partner initiatives, and interviews. Pro gamers are expected to behave in a professional manner and conform to other requirements outlined in their contracts. This is a necessary part of becoming a pro gamer. Without the generation of revenue, it would not be profitable to pursue gaming as a career.

The world's greatest players have earnt more than $1 million in winnings to date. Amateur-level players may not receive a set wage or even a contract, instead they will usually take a share of the prize pool from any tournaments they participate in. It is worth noting that playing at a lower level can provide valuable experience and contacts that could help develop their career.

A key component of becoming an esports pro is your ability to play a game. You need to be able to be good within your discipline to make real waves. Moreover, there are a number of other things that a gamer should consider when trying to make a career as an esports pro. A strategy should be thought about in terms of your focus, goal orientation and approach. Knowledge of the business of esports and the basic principles of how to maximise your gaming performance is also beneficial. Going further, the ability to market yourself could help develop your pro gamer career. If you can imbed yourself within the community and actively put yourself out there, you maybe scouted by a top team.

The dynamics and youth of the esports industry means that that the landscape is and will continue to change for the foreseeable future. The road to becoming a pro gamer and staying at the top will continue to be challenging, but motivation, strategy and a strong mind-set will be paramount in success.

Like any career, you will have to put hours into your specialism. You need to practice regularly to gain the extensive game knowledge and elite mechanical skills and reflexes to compete against the best.

Esports Consultants

A career as an esports consultant involves helping organisations and individuals understand the more complex aspects of working within the nascent industry. Furthermore, esport consultants will help aspiring teams, players and organisations to identify a strategy to build their brand and help organisations develop solutions to increase growth. As an esports consultant, you would help to develop the esports scene by providing advice to the organisations that drive the industry. Often, as an esports consultant, you would provide expert advice in a particular area in which you have a wide knowledge of the subject matter.

The role of an esports consultant is particularly important with gamers as they are just gamers. They can be taken advantage of as they often will not know better. Consultants within esports need to help those within the space better understand the industry.

There are opportunities to become internal or external esports consultants. Internal consultants would be someone who operates within an organisation but is available to be consulted on areas of their specialisation by other departments or individuals. In contrast, external consultants are those who are employed externally to the client, often via a consulting firm or agency. They often provide their expertise on a temporary basis, usually for a fee. Regardless, by utilising a consultant, clients and organisations have access to deeper levels of expertise. Hiring an external consultant provides this access at a financially feasible level compared to retaining an in-house consultant on a long-term basis.

Esports Lawyers

As the industry matures, more law firms will focus on the industry. Esports lawyers are fundamental in for players, teams, game developers and other organisations within the space. These lawyers would handle contract negotiations, team negotiations, sponsorship and endorsements, team mediation and athlete representation. Esport lawyers provide support for the different stakeholders within the industry, aiming to create legal solutions for constantly evolving sets of challenges.

It is important to have good, solid contracts so that everything that is expected is clear. This is particularly the case for players. As will be discussed in the legal issues aspect of the next section, individuals with legal background will be paramount for the direction and growth of the industry. They are crucial to making the competitive gaming industry a better and fairer place.

Esports Agents

As in traditional sports, an esports agent is someone who looks after a player's best interests, usually taking commission on deals and contracts secured. The role entails aspects such as securing sponsorship deals, handling the players image or negotiating better contracts for the player.

Additionally, an agent usually represents the player, handling the paperwork and legal aspects of their career – this is essential to enable the player to focus on playing and performing well in the virtual world. Furthermore, good agents would be able to handle some elements of coaching, public relations, events and marketing. As they would need to liaise with team owners, managers, coaches and other individuals, an esports agent needs to be well networked.

Esports agents essentially act as a legal representative for professional esports figures like athletes, managers and coaches. They are to offer strategic advice and representation, by procuring and negotiating employment and endorsement deals. As the role is contract centric, a background in contract law would be beneficial.

Esports Journalists

An esports journalist gathers and analyses information to create content that is engaging and in the public interest. As an esport journalist, you can publish on a wide variety of mediums, such as newspapers and online. A career in esport journalism would require written news stories, analysis articles, opinion pieces, interviews of players and other people in the industry, as well as match reports.

Senior editors would usually have the responsibility for choosing which stories to cover, assigning tasks to different members of the team, proof reading and editing, and providing the focus of a piece.

Building relationships is very important in journalism as having close contacts and industry insiders enables early access to stories and developments before others. Accuracy of information and objectiveness is also fundamental in journalism.

Esports Content Creators

A career as an esports content creator is similar in some respects to journalism. The main distinction is the fact that a content creator role is less news-focussed or objective, and more entertainment focussed.

The content will usually be focussed on a specific area rather than a broad audience, and can be in various forms from written to visual. Examples of content creators include; internal news writers for a specific team or game developer and content creators for YouTubers and streamers. Additionally, brands or sponsors might want to produce a series of promotional content around esports with a humorous style to attract a certain demographic.

The digital age and nature of esports has resulted in vast amount of opportunities to create content within the esports space, particularly in a video format. This is evident by the numbers on Twitch and YouTube, in terms of viewers. The ability to shoot, edit and produce videos to a professional level is a skill set that is in high demand. Video content is a highly effective method to promote players, teams and organisations. Additionally, written content provides for a strategy to create significant volume of content, at a low cost.

As the space grows, there will be a much larger demand for content creators. Content creating a good way to enter the esports space as you will become an integral part of the community, dedicated to progressing the space.

Event Managers

This role is similar to that of a project manager or product manager, but with a greater focus on events or a series of events. A career in esports event managing would entail being responsible for ensuring a tournament or esports event is a success. Success in this role can be measured by viewer numbers, ticket sales and positive reception from fans and the press.

An event manager role in esports is incredibly varied, with the requirement to liaise with various teams. These include the production team, partners stakeholders, venue management, marketing and sales to name a few.

As an events manager, you would need to manage a team, budgets and timescales, research venues and suppliers, hire equipment and contractors and take health and safety into consideration. Additionally, as more companies seek to promote their products within esports, event managers will be required to organise activities with these organisations.

Community Manager

A community manager career would entail looking after a community of a game, esport, tournament provider or other area of gaming. This will be achieved through engaging with and responding to the community on social media. Ideally, community managers would work closely with the Public Relations and Marketing teams. This is primarily because what a community manager says and does affects the audience's perception in relation to a product or brand.

Additionally, a community manager role would entail writing press releases, conducting interviews and identifying key requests and reactions from the community and feeding them back to the team.

Sales/Account Manager

A career in esports sales would involve selling a particular product, service, event or initiative. As an esports sales executive or account manager, you would play a big part in striking deals and generating revenue. The fundamental aspects of the role include customer acquisition, building relationships with key customers and partners, hitting targets and negotiating costs.

Role could involve, for example, selling online advertising space or esports tournament sponsorship packages to brands, event ticket sales and merchandise. If you have the gift of the gab and a passion for gaming and esports, sales could be an easy way to break into the industry.

Public Relations (PR) & Marketing

PR is all about managing the flow of information from an organisation to the public. A career in PR entails securing positive coverage with publications and other influencers in order to grow the company's reputation. This is extremely important to help grow the business, the fanbase and improve the public perception of the brand.

A career in marketing is like PR, but will usually have a budget that can be used on advertising. The overall aim of the role is to promote a business and increase sales of its products and services. For example, a brand may want their marketer to advertise with streaming platforms or esports teams to market its products to the young demographic.

There are a wide range of areas within marketing, from social media to sponsorships, partnerships, brand image, slogans, adverts to name a few.

Team/Organisation Managers

A manager of a team or organisation will be required to look after all aspects of how an esports company or team operates. This includes the responsibility of hiring staff, deciding which games and tournaments to take part in, marketing and business strategy, paying wages, partnerships, the company ethos and direction and much more. The manager may delegate some of these tasks to others.

Team Staff

Behind every great esports team, there will be staff that will help train and get the best out of the players. A coach and analyst are two key roles that are influential on a team's performance. If you love playing, competition and the constant struggle to improve and drive to be the best, then a team coach may be for you. If you like, and are good with numbers and statistics, then an analyst role may be ideal for you.

Like traditional sports, an esport coach helps to train the team against other teams, with the goal of improving and winning. They work closely with players to help motivate them, identify their strengths and weaknesses, while at the same time ensuring they are playing at their best.

Furthermore, the role as a coach entails analysing opponents and developing strategies to win as many matches and tournament as possible. They may be required to record matches, watch them, analyse, make notes and develop strategies to improve the team's performance. A coach also provides training in certain aspects of the game, such as macro-based decision making. As a result, up to date knowledge of the game is fundamental.

Esports analysts take information and use it to provide interesting stats and extrapolate valuable analysis from them. This can be for a team, tournament provider or game developer. Esports team analysts often work closely with coaches to help generate strategies, analyse strengths and weaknesses, and to then communicate these to the players. This done well, would bring out the best in the players and the team. Some individuals can be responsible for both coaching and analyst duties.

Companies and developers employ analysts and statisticians to keep track of facts and other game information throughout the season.

Broadcasters/Production

Within an esports event team, there is the Broadcaster and Production department who handle a wide range of activities. These include camera work, lighting and ensuring the streaming, screens and speaker set up are working. The Broadcaster and Production crew will ensure that everything is displayed correctly to the viewer.

Video Production staff may be required to record additional interviews before the event and edit them in.

Commentators

Within the esports world, commentators are known as a
shoutcaster or host. A career as a commentator entails
speaking over the action to inform and entertain the viewer.
Naturally, you would need good knowledge of the game and
the teams they are casting. Their role within esports is similar
to that of traditional commentators and TV presenters at times.
It is all about putting the show together and offering
personality to bring the match to life.

Admin/Referee –

A career as an admin or esports referee would entail recording
the outcome of the matches, making sure that players stick to
the rules and hand out penalties if they are broken.
Additionally, an admin may be required to help resolve any
in-game or technical issues, such as a PC freezing mid-

tournament. Consequently, they will need to know the game and the tournament's rulebook inside out. This will enable an admin to enforce the rules and avoid any controversies or unfair decisions. Role is like that of a referee in traditional sports.

Esports Recruitment & Human Resources (HR)

As with any industry, there will be organisations that will require recruiting specific individuals – whether to replace or grow and scale. There will naturally be movement of individuals from one organisation to another within esports. Furthermore, there will be others that will want to embark on a career within esports.

Recruitment, in a nutshell, is about finding the best people for the job. They will often work on behalf of a client to find a suitable person for a specific job role. Recruiting is often outsourced by the company to third-party recruitment agencies. The service fee is usually obtained through charging the clients (companies that are hiring), not the individual.

Recruitment has not become standardised in esports yet as the industry is still in its infancy and there are still a few hurdles to overcome. In time, as esports matures and professionalises, there will be a greater demand for jobs and hence the esports recruitment industry will thrive.

Human Resources (HR) is usually the internal department within a company that looks after staff, settles disputes, arrange employee benefits and are responsible for people management. They aim to ensure the staff are happy, and law-abiding.

5.3 Challenges in Esports

Despite the growth and success in esports over the years, problems do exist within the industry. Particularly due to the digital nature of games and the infancy of the industry, there are a range of challenges that need to be noted. In this section, I will outline the key challenges and issues that the esports industry faces.

<u>Legal Issues</u>

Given the immaturity of the industry, it is apparent that there is no clear legal framework and hence significant uncertainty within esports. In Europe, France have regulated in some form. They have established the professional scene of esports in the country, moving esports away from the concept of traditional sports. Despite France's move in the positive direction, the general global consensus is lack of regulation, meaning that, in practice, general provisions of law are being used.

The creation of rules and regulation must be approached with caution. A bad or over-regulatory framework can result in a negative impact on the development of the dynamic industry. On the other hand, a good regulatory framework could provide the esports with the ability to positively economically impact the entertainment sector in the 21st century.

When considering the legal issues faced in esports, it is important to consider the key components of the industry, primarily the key players. By just focussing on game publishers, competition organisers, teams and players – the key legal issues become apparent.

The publishers are the main players within the industry. They hold the power as they hold the ownership of the intellectual and industrial property of video games. Game publishers decide who, when and under what conditions can organise a competition around their product. There is a fundamental reliance on the publishers in any case in order to carry out the esports economic activity. This dominance can result in competitive advantage over the other parties, for example, when the publishers decide to become the organisers of the competition. The main legal relationship of the publishers is with the event producers, by authorising them to use their game in the competitions. The owners of the video game must formally give up the intellectual property rights, in order to exploit the audio-visual rights of the competitions.

The competition organisers or event producers are responsible for designing and organising the tournaments. Naturally, these promoters have a direct relationship with all participants in the industry. They must obtain permission from the publisher and establish the competition rules that directly affect the teams registered. The economic investment made by the event producers are often recuperated by commercialising the audio-visual rights of the competition and seeking sponsorships. Additionally, event producers need to be able to ensure integrity of the competition by implementing anti-doping and anti-match fixing measures derived from betting. As a result of all these elements, producers need to consider a wide range of legal situations in order to be able to carry out their activity with guarantees.

Teams, on the other hand, are entities that hire players to represent them in tournaments. Teams are often established in a specific legal form, depending on the degree of professionalisation and the competitions in which they participate. Certain competitions require teams to have a certain legal form. For example, in Spain, most teams participating in official competitions have the form of a limited liability company. This is primarily because there is no specific legal entity to regulate the teams' economic activity otherwise. As the industry matures, more teams will become professionalised and incorporate coaches, community managers, psychologists and physiotherapists into their structures.

Esports players are a central component of the industry and could be defined as a professional video game player who competes within the scope of an association or company, in exchange for remuneration. France have the only regulation that provides a specific status to esports players. Professional gamers often have legal relationships with teams, producers and sponsors. Within player contracts, it is paramount for players to resolve the transfer of their image rights. In addition to their employment contracts, players may be subject to certain risks such as injuries, and so these must be addressed to provide them with the necessary coverage.

The key legal concern for these key esports entities is whether the laws and provisions we already have are sufficient for all the legal relationships or, instead, we require specific regulation. They key point to consider in answering this concern would be whether or not, in all the legal relationships within esports, one of the parties is in a dominant position. If this is the case, then it could lead to abusive conditions for the rest.

As a sector that has complex legal relationships, the industry is exposed to anti-competitive practices, conflicts of interests and collusive agreements. Participants can impose their own rules on other individuals based on their dominant position. This can jeopardise the integrity of the competition and esports itself. Moreover, this can be valid justification for public intervention in protecting the public interest and the parties that may be de facto placed at disadvantage within the sector.

I think it is more important for the authorities to be aware of the issues in case intervention is needed. In time, there will need a clear legal framework to provide certainty and regulation within the industry. There are three ways that a framework could be put in place:

1. Mixture of industry self-regulation and general provisions of local laws in each member country – This is the current option.

2. Sector specific regulation in which all aspects of economic activity are regulated, or only those that require public intervention to ensure legal certainty and the balance of rights – This is the option chosen by France.

3. The consideration of esports as a sport and therefore application of specific regulations in the field of sports.

I personally think that the sector specific regulations would be the best way to approach the legal issues within esports. The only concern is that the industry is evolving at a phenomenal rate, meaning that the regulation may become obsolete in a short space of time.

Cheating & Corruption

The Esports Integrity Coalition (ESIC) identified four main threats to esports, in terms of corruption, as:

- Cheating to win using software cheats
- Online cyber-attacks to slow or disable an opponent (DDoS attacks)
- Match-fixing

- Doping

ESIC has attempted to deal with these threats by publishing a participants' Code of Conduct, Anti-Corruption Code and an Anti-Doping Policy. These aim to deal with all the significant threats they identified as all members who join must follow the codes. There is a unified disciplinary procedure for anything that offends the code of ethics.

Cyber Attacks

Despite the ESIC taking steps to combat corruption and cheating, esports can be susceptible to cyber-attacks. For example, a Distributed Denial of Service attack (DDoS) can occur where the attacker sends countless requests to communicate with the victim's internet. Consequentially, the victim's internet is unable to perform operations for a period of time. Within esports, DDoS attacks can be used to kick opposing gamers off the internet during a match.

The industry needs to deal with this distinct problem as it threatens the integrity and legitimacy of competitions, however the attacks are often untraceable. The best method to protect the industry against cyber-attacks would be to enforce strict policy in relation to cyber-crimes and cheating. Going further, it would be worthwhile educating the youth regarding the consequences of cheating and cyber-attacks to themselves and the industry.

Virtual violence

The violent nature of many video games is perceived to be a negative influence on the young consumers of the market. Games like Grand Theft Auto IV have been said to encourage acts depicted in the game, from robbery to murder. Although

GTA IV is not generally considered a major esport title, other titles such as Call of Duty and Halo may attract the same negative opinions.

This issue was highlighted by the International Olympic Committee in their recent discussion of whether to include esports in the 2024 Olympics. In response to this obstacle, I would simply refer individuals to other activities that could lead to real life violence. Take boxing, UFC and Rugby for example. These are contact sports that are 'violent' in nature. All I would say is that the age indicators for games should be adhered to by parents and guardians.

It is only a matter of time before mainstream media notices how particularly violent some games are. Titles like Counter-Strike are significantly graphic – and more importantly, seem much more realistic. The correlation between violent video games and real-life violence have been drawn before. It is inevitable that this challenge will face more coverage, as the massive young audiences drawn to esports is further noticed.

Stereotyping of Gamers

There are several misconceptions about gamers. They are highlighted as solitary creatures who prefer communicating via headsets and through screens rather than in person or as a community. Gamers are viewed as individuals who are significantly unhealthy due to staring at a screen for eight hours a day. Additionally, there is the stereotype brush that paints gaming as a platform to breed violence, drugs, theft and truancy.

The negative views and public opinion regarding gaming culture is well known. This stereotyping is unfair and due to the actions of a few individuals and media propaganda. Moreover, in relation to lifestyles of gamers, I work in an office for a FTSE 250 company and spend eight hours on a chair staring at a screen. What is the difference in terms of activity between my current job and the career of a pro gamer? The same way you would need to spend hours on your chair in an office role, you would need to spend on your chair gaming.

The influence of sponsors and mainstream media within the esports industry has positively influenced the perception of video games, particularly in North America. In order to combat this challenge, coordination between mainstream media and esports organisations can be utilised to shift the perception of the industry towards a more positive image.

Addiction

Esport players spend a lot of time playing video games and practicing for competitions, often up to 10 hours a day. This commitment is like the time spent by athlete's playing traditional established sports.

Some studies have documented that spending prolonged time playing video games often leads to video game addiction, as well as adverse social and psychological effects. I guess that is the same with doughnuts, McDonalds and many other things that are not good in excess. I personally think that addiction is not a valid reason for prohibiting the activity, but health effects are.

For that reason, I feel it is important to educate consumers as to the potential consequences of increased video game use. This proactive approach would ensure that participants are not experiencing any adverse health effects, and hence avoid any future issues.

Underage Gambling

Furthermore, there are a number of places where cash-equivalent items can be wagered, such as skins for guns. Esports is growing exponentially, but underage gambling is a major concern that could jeopardise the wellbeing of the industry. There are stories of kids stealing and spending thousands of pounds of their parents' money. As esports betting rises in frequency, it is just a matter of time until the government starts noticing and implementing rules and regulations.

Instability

There is a great deal of instability within esports presently. This issue is in relation to game titles, competitions, teams and players, to name a few.

This instability is limiting the growth of the space as many sponsors are weary of shelling out big bucks for a team or organisation that can potentially become defunct after a short space of time.

Game titles have a life span, or tend to. Often, games that were popular ten or fifteen years ago, are no longer in the gaming scene.

Player Salaries

For an industry that serves as advertising for other industries that take home several billion dollars of revenue per year, the player salaries are horrendously low, generally speaking. Particularly considering players are pinnacle to the success of the industry, low player salaries are a real challenge to esports.

Player Representation

In line with player salaries, there are also issues of representation. A significant number of pros lack even basic representation. Despite there being large organisations aiming at representing players, the general trend is that pros, particularly amateurs, represent themselves or are represented by their families.

Players really need professional representation – agents and lawyers – at all levels. For the same reasons you see representation in traditional sports, professional representation is fundamental for pro gamers. Other parties that the player will contract with will have legal representation, such as team lawyers that draft up the player contracts. The only way to ensure fair agreements and a counterbalance for contracts is to have somebody representing the player.

Longevity of game titles.

Additionally, I could see professional gamers streaming their practice sessions less as they try to conceal their tactics from opposition. This could cause potential problems in terms of viewership and engagement in the future.

Chapter 6: The Future of Esports

The future of esports is looking extremely exciting. With the possibility of inclusion in the 2024 Olympics, huge developments within the space and further improvements to technology – esports is clearly an industry and entertainment activity that should be watched with an intent eye. In this chapter, I will discuss what needs to happen in the esports industry going forward, whether esports will feature in the Olympics in 2024, and what the future of esports might look like.

6.1 Esports – The Next Olympic Sport?

The 6th Olympic Summit took place on the 28th October 2017, in Lausanne, where the International Olympic Committee (IOC) and the representatives of the Olympic Movement met.

Many topics which were important to the future of the Olympic Movement were discussed, but the scope of this article will revolve around the discussion in relation to the development of eGames/esports.

What was Concluded at The Olympic Summit

The Summit concluded:

- Esports are showing significant growth, particularly within the youth demographic across numerous countries.
- Esports can provide a platform for engagement with the Olympic Movement.
- Competitive esports can be considered a sporting activity
- To be recognised by the IOC as a sport, the content of esports must not infringe on the Olympic values
- A further requirement for recognition by the IOC must be the existence of an organisation guaranteeing compliance with the rules and regulations of the Olympic Movement (anti-doping, betting, manipulation and etc).

The Summit asked the IOC, together with the Global Association of International Sports Federation (GAISF), to begin a dialogue with the gaming industry and players to explore this area further. The outcome of this 'exploration' will be provided to the Olympic Movement stakeholders in due course.

It is important to note that the Summit concluded that competitive esports could be considered as a sporting activity as the players involved prepare and train with an intensity which can be comparable to athletes in traditional sports. The Summit also concluded that esports is an avenue for the Olympic Movement to increase engagement among the youth across the globe. Two promising conclusions for the inclusion of esports in the 2024 Olympics.

Nevertheless, the Olympic Governing body did set out two clear prerequisites for esports' inclusion in the Olympic Games:

1. The content of esports must not infringe Olympic Values.

2. There must be a global governing body that can guarantee compliance with the rules and regulations of the Olympic Movement.

Olympic Values

The goal of the Olympic Movement is to contribute to building a peaceful and better world by educating youth through sport practiced without discrimination of any kind and in accordance with Olympism and its values. This requires mutual understanding with a spirit of friendship, solidarity and fair play.

The Core Olympic Values include:

- Friendship

- Respect

- Excellence

- Non-discrimination

- Peace

I believe that this stipulation relates to the content of the games in determining what becomes an Olympic event and what does not. Two months ago, IOC President Thomas Bach made a few points on the topic:

"We want to promote non-discrimination, non-violence, and peace among people. This doesn't match with video games, which are about violence, explosions and killing. And there we have to draw a clear line."

This could mean that some of the major esports titles are a no go; including League of Legends, Dota-2, Counter-strike and Overwatch. Esports resembling sports that are played in real life, such as football and basketball, would be more likely to be acceptable.

That being said, it is strange that these games are called out for being too violent, but Olympic sports like boxing and shooting are allowed. I guess graphic violent titles where killing and explosions are focal in the game, like Counter-strike, is the key concern.

Some have a concern that 'nobody will watch' the Olympic esport debut the major 'violent' titles were left out. This is most likely due to two eligible global best sellers (FIFA and NBA 2K) not making it in the top 10 lists for numerous number-tracking services for Twitch.

Admittedly, there is a lack of eSport viewership for titles such as FIFA and NBA 2K, however, in my opinion there is much more to it. It is not as simple as inferring, for example, that there are not people who would watch a FIFA at the Olympics.

The esports industry is very young and as these segments mature and the infrastructure develops, the viewership will increase significantly.

Global Esports Governing Body

There has been a real call for a more organised global governing body within esports for some time now. This stipulation reaffirms the need for a recognised regulatory body. At this moment in time, it really is the 'wild west' in terms of governing bodies.

The International esports Federation (IeSF) is probably the most developed governing body, growing from 9 eSport associations in 2008 to 47-member nations currently. It aims to promote esports and its players, and to standardise the industry.

Additionally, the World eSport Association (WESA) was founded in 2016 by the esports veterans, ESL, along with many esport teams. Founding members include big names such as Fnatic, Ninjas in Pyjamas and G2 Esports. It is another organisation that aims to set standards, help bring consistency and regulation to competitions, and organise the broader world of esports. The Esports Integrity Coalition (ESIC), as alluded to earlier, also intend to establish a standard for ethics in esports. They aim to be responsible for preventing cheating and corruption.

Despite the existence of these associations and bodies, there remains no real official global governing body that standardises the rules and regulations across the whole industry. I think that the lack of a real global governing body is simply due to the age of the esports industry. Despite the history of the industry tracing back to the '80s and '90s, esports is still very much in its conception. I firmly believe that a governing body which will unify the industry on a global level is only around the corner.

Will Esports Feature in the Olympics?

Competitive video gaming has generated over $600m in revenue in 2017, has a global audience of over 380 million, and will be included in the 2022 Asian Games. There is a lot to be excited about. Whether it makes it to the 2024 Olympics will depend on the development of esports over the next few years, particularly with the esports resembling sports played in real life. Whether esports needs the Olympics is a totally different question.

Esports can and will grow without featuring in the Olympics, but the inclusion as a medal event would provide recognition to the industry. It would definitely be beneficial for the industry in all sorts of ways.

In my humble opinion, I think FIFA 24 may very well feature in the Olympic Games in Paris. The growth of the FIFA esport market has been phenomenal over the last few years and shows no real signs of slowing. I think it may be in the form of the emerging 'Pro Clubs' mode.

Furthermore, I think it is only a matter of time before a global governing body is created for esports that unifies the laws to make it fair and clear to all within the industry. The development of this global body will also set the foundations for the future expansion of esports. Once this occurs, transition into an Olympic activity will be much easier.

The 2024 Programme will start to become shaped in 2019, and a decision on what sports will be added in Paris will be made after the 2020 Games in Tokyo.

6.2 What Needs to Happen in the Esports Industry

For sustainable and swift growth within the UK esports industry, there must be strategies in place that play to the industries strengths. A recent YouGov study has recently put the UK at the bottom of the table when compared to China, the US, Germany and more. The proposals I have suggested will be hugely beneficial for the UK esports industry, on a national and global level. It could also be transferrable to other regions.

Importance of Engaging with Viewers

Non-endemic sponsors and investors have been a fundamental ingredient for the exponential growth of esports in North America. This needs to be replicated in the UK. Increased sponsorship and investment within the industry can only be achieved through increased viewership and popularity. Consequently, this would result in sustainable and significant revenue growth.

A few ways to increase viewership and engagement, particularly within the UK:

- National Esport Division Systems –This would be excellent in propelling viewership to untold heights.
- Increased Number of Player Contracts: Increase in esport player contracts would provide stability to the team's roster, resulting in increased fans and public

engagement. Think about football teams. If a team changed their players every week, how could you possibly develop relationships and grow attachment to a player?

- Improved Investment, Streaming and Marketing: These elements need to be improved to increase viewership in the UK. Success in the industry lies with a supportive, educated and involved fan base.

- Celebrity Endorsement of the Industry: With public icons endorsing the industry, whether by owning a team or competing themselves, viewership and engagement would significantly increase.

- Increase in Cash Prizes: Increased cash rewards for competitions will result in increased viewership. If a tournament was played for £10,000 or £1,000,000 – which do you think would receive more viewers?

- Increased Accessibility to the Esports Industry – More players need to be given the opportunity to access the esports industry.

National Esport Division Systems

There needs to be national esport leagues with a division system, similarly to football. With exclusive spots in the top division, esport teams would have to work their way up to the top tier. This in turn would lead to a proliferation of esport teams, in a bid to reap the huge financial benefits.

This national league system will result in the inevitable upsurge of viewers and consequently non-endemic sponsors. Sponsors will be drawn to esport teams and players within the UK. Who would pass up on the opportunity to sponsor a team in the top division of a national league that will play in front of millions?

Non-endemic organisations will sponsor lower tier teams that have opportunity, in a hope they make it to the top division. Teams and players will also be valued much higher, resulting in the further investment into teams and grassroots esport support. At Intergalactic Gaming, we intend to launch a national UK esport league within the coming months.

Improved Marketing and Streaming of Events:

There are various ways that events can be marketed and streamed for increased viewership and engagement. From simple elements, such as the commentating on matches, the esports industry needs to develop this area significantly to attract more viewers. For Intergalactic Gaming, we have devised several unique methods to market and stream our events to optimise engagement. For example, by creating a narrative, engagement and viewership will naturally increase as fans will have more of an affinity with teams and players.

Another example could be involving UK Universities in the world of esports. You only need to look to the University of British Columbia (UBC) in Canada to see some of the benefits. They opened an esports space in 2016 and invested in its UBC Esports Gaming Club, boasting 800 members. Around 50 of these members compete at a high level, winning more than $500,000 from esport tournaments so far! In the USA, esport scholarships are now being provided for students.

Esport brands need to create a dedicated strategy and retain control over their revenue models, as opposed to creating simple strategies and badging exercises. There needs to be self-sustaining strategies to operate and run effective esports programmes locally and globally. How to approach creating such a strategy needs to be educated. It is fantastic to see a

UK University (Staffordshire) launching an esports degree in 2018.

Celebrity Endorsement of the Esport Industry:

Celebrity endorsement always has a profound influence on public trends. A celebrity endorsing a game, product, service or industry would be hugely beneficial. Their fan base would become aware and often follow suit. Celebrity endorsement was and is one of the key driving factors for the success of many products, such as Beats Headphones. More relevantly, I recall discovering many famous celebrities endorsing the game; World of Warcraft. Celebrities such as Vin Diesel, Mr T, Mila Kunis, Chuck Norris, and many more made me more inclined to want to play the game.

The same applies for the esport industry. Celebrities endorsing the industry, in most forms, would result in increased engagement within the industry. Traditional sport teams and entrepreneurs like Shaquille O'Neal (former basketball pro) and the Philadelphia 76ers (basketball team) have moved into esports over the years in the USA. A few months ago, Zlatan Ibrahimović (Man Utd football player) also invested in an esports start-up based in Sweden. We need public figures investing within the UK esports industry.

Increased Number of Player Contracts

It provides security and benefits to both parties. It allows players to be guaranteed rights and welfare. It allows players to protect themselves. For the organisation, it provides a form of stability from their greatest assets, their players, facilitating the building of a more stable roster. The stable roster consequently results in more fan and public engagement, team identity and a narrative around the organisation and its players.

Furthermore, the player contract demonstrates the value the organisation places on the players and indicates sophistication to the industry. It provides real professionalism, driving the social stigma attached to avid gamers away. Unfortunately, gamers can be viewed as 'nerds that stay in their room all day and play games all day'. This contract system will provide credibility to esport players and increase their image within society. Of course, player contracts do exist, but they need to be rolled out on a larger scale within the UK.

Increased in Cash Prizes

This can be achieved via methods such as sponsored tournaments or decentralised large prize pool tournaments. The desirable demographics and characteristics of the viewers (millennials) would provide huge benefits to the industry, such as increased sponsorship and prize pools.

This financial incentive would result in a consequential proliferation of esport players, esport teams, investors, sponsors and viewers. More people will get into the industry, whether it is viewing matches or competing.

Increased Accessibility to the Esports Industry

Presently, it is difficult for players to break into the esport industry and become professional gamers. The possible cause of this could be because of the infant nature of the industry. This means infrequent tournaments and lack of awareness within the community. More gamers need to be given routes to becoming esport professionals through education, awareness and opportunity.

At Intergalactic Gaming, we have developed a unique strategy to increase accessibility for gamers, regardless of skill.

Conclusion

The YouGov study does put us at the bottom of the six countries that were surveyed, but it does not tell the whole picture. Awareness of esports within the UK rises from 35% to 64% when you concentrate on adults aged 18 to 24. When looking at all male respondents, just under half are aware of esports.

There is no doubt that in the coming years, as the millennials grow older, esports will continue to grow. Despite this, there needs to be strategies in place to ensure that we have sustainable growth. Additionally, these strategies can be implemented to augment the UK esport industry. I look forward to drive things forward with Intergalactic Gaming Ltd!

6.3 The Future of Esports

It may be a career many kids and teenagers dream of, but as of now, it is clearly not a profitable one (apart from players who literally dominate in their game). Although top League of Legend players have contracts with quite promising salaries, we all know they do not get to stay on the top forever. Either way, it is extremely difficult to make a name and succeed in esports. I believe that the requirements to succeed in esports are not only hours of practice and absolute dedication, but also pure talent.

The industry is booming and will gain global traction over the coming years. The future is bright and exponential. Teams are managed and ran like any other sports teams. In the future there will be well established career paths in the industry, whereas in the past, being a competitive gamer was not even considered a career. Currently, however, it is not a profitable career for gamers unless one literally dominates their chosen game to compete in.

One thing that the popularity of esports has done is open the doors to opportunity for more developers. As with any trend or genre, once big games create a space, small developers can enter that space and find their place within it - a place that didn't exist not so long ago.

The future of esports looks like it will be made even more interesting with immersive technology, such as Virtual Reality (VR). As these immersive technologies develop, esports will be transformed and the industry will no doubt flourish. For many games, such as Dota-2, we even have VR viewing modes that literally put you as an observer in the battlefield during a match.

At the Intel Extreme Masters in Oakland. Intel created product suites for gamers to demo on the arena floor and activated experiences in virtual reality. The matches were broadcast online to 360-degree viewers and VR headsets and attendees were able to view the live tournaments at viewing stations around the venue.

In conclusion, esports does have an extremely bright future thanks to the copious amount of both casual and competitive players worldwide, although aspiring to be a professional gamer is very risky and insecure. At some point soon, it is highly likely that eSports will be recognised as a true sport.

Chapter 7: Conclusion

The esports ecosystem truly represents a unique manifestation of traditional sport development through a digital medium. New elements of competition increasing the potential for skill development and mastery have been introduced over the years through the evolution of video games. From coin-operated arcade games to team-based objective games, video gaming began as a recreational activity fulfilling the intrinsic need to be entertained to a more competitive scene.

Social interaction has also developed over the years and has played a critical role in the valorisation of video games, increasing the level of competition between gamers.

While the esport ecosystem benefits from traditional sport development elements, unique problems exist that threaten the image and integrity of competition. As more attention is drawn to the growing industry, educated sports managers may involve themselves with the systems' operations as it progresses towards a visible mainstream sport system.

The future of esports does look extremely exciting. It is one to watch over the coming years as the industry evolves and matures. In my eyes, there is no doubt that this industry will grow exponentially, to the stage that it outcompetes majority of the established traditional sports.

Chapter 8: Intergalactic Gaming

8.1 Context

This chapter is a 'bonus' chapter in which I would like to briefly provide context as to how and why I entered the esports space many years ago.

Around 4 years ago, whilst at University, I was playing FIFA, and as usual was winning. Then the inspiration hit. The light bulb switched on. I thought, why could I not earn money by playing FIFA? Why could I not play someone with similar skill to me for money?

I immediately turned to google to see if my golden idea had already been done. It did turn out that the core idea had already been converted to reality by a company based in America. I refused to give up the idea as I still felt it was an incredibly niche market and that company was experiencing significant growth. I also felt that this provider was not really engaging for the FIFA community and had many flaws.

I went up to Newcastle to see my friend and business partner, Josh, to discuss the idea with him. He loved it and we got brainstorming over the weekend. We did our due diligence and touched on esports, putting together a business plan in 2014.

Following from this, we went hunting for finance. Having seen the business plan recently, I understand why our hunt for finance failed. It was terrible. The concept was not complete, and the business plan was written poorly, dare I say rushed. We put the business on hold, keeping a keen eye on the market and going through the motions at University.

In the final year of University, I had an opportunity to bring out the old business plan and discuss the idea with another friend. He loved the idea and, again, we got to brainstorming and mental simulating. The esports and FIFA market had evolved significantly from the conception of the business idea in 2014. This was the time to go for it!

Since graduating from University in June 2017, me and my business partner got to work. Following the markets evolve over several years and armed with our increased bank of experience, we were able to create a new and significantly more formidable business plan. A plan that described and outlined a business that will propel the esports industry forward in a creative and innovative manner.

We have designed a sustainable ecosystem that will add value and support to the esports infrastructure. Our idea is simple. We intend to target the FIFA esports market primarily with our uniquely devised model, essentially acting as esports event producers, team owners and agents.

8.2 The Idea & Vision

The vision for Intergalactic Gaming is to lead the drive for FIFA to be categorised as a top esports title. By providing a platform for players of all skill levels, we intend to increase the accessibility and awareness of esports.

This vision will be achieved through our carefully crafted ecosystem that will provide FIFA players with an unparalleled experience. Intergalactic Gaming will provide gamers with the ability to compete in various game modes on our platform, while engaging with other gamers around the world.

Our freemium model will enable users to try out our basic features before committing to our premium service. The money from subscriptions will go back into our ecosystem, providing more value for our customers.

Sources

Nielsen Report, The Esports Playbook: Maximising investment through understanding the fans, October 2017

NewZoo Report, The Global Esports Market Report 2017, February 2017

Business Insiders Report, The eSports Ecosystem, March 2017

History & Analysis of Esport Systems, Tyler. L Snavely, 2014

Chandler, M. (2014). Professional video gamers gaining sponsors, viewers; E-Sports popularity growing; some elite pro gamers earning six figures, but careers over by mid-20s. Investor's Business Daily. Retrieved from www.lexisnexis.com/hottopics/lnacademic

Financial Times, Esports is the gaming business ready to come of age? November 2017 https://www.ft.com/content/ef8539b6-be2a-11e7-9836-b25f8adaa111

IBC365, Is it time to enter the eSports arena? November 2017 https://www.ibc.org/production/how-big-is-the-esports-opportunity/2533.article

IHS Markit, Global Market for Esports Video is Booming, May 2017, http://news.ihsmarkit.com/press-release/technology/global-market-esports-video-booming-china-leading-way-ihs-markit-reports

Market Realist, How Esports Could Transform Activision, September 2017, http://marketrealist.com/2017/09/how-esports-could-transform-activision/ http://marketrealist.com/search/?search_term=esports (other articles from Market Realist)

Sports Business Daily, Esports' millennial appeal proving to entice once weary sponsors across sports industry
https://www.sportsbusinessdaily.com/Daily/Issues/2017/11/10/Esports-Rising/Millennial.aspx

Adage, Are you game? E.J Schultz
http://adage.com/article/news/e-sports/308447/

Deloitte Global, eSports: Bigger and smaller than you think, 2016
https://www2.deloitte.com/global/en/pages/technology-media-and-telecommunications/articles/tmt-pred16-media-esports-bigger-smaller-than-you-think.html

PwC, Esports Key Findings: Segments Insights
https://www.pwc.com/gx/en/industries/entertainment-media/outlook/segment-insights/e-sports.html

Telegraph, What are esports? A Beginners Guide, October 2017
http://www.telegraph.co.uk/gaming/guides/esports-beginners-guide/

Fortune, Big brands gravitating towards esports, July 2014
http://fortune.com/2014/07/24/esports-sponsors/

Asian Review, Esports reach big time in China, November 2017, https://asia.nikkei.com/Business/Trends/Esports-reach-big-time-in-China

BBC, IOC Considering Esports for Future Games, October 2017 http://www.bbc.co.uk/sport/olympics/41790148

Event Marketer, How Live Events and Sponsorships are elevating the Booming Esports Industry, March 2017 http://www.eventmarketer.com/article/cover-story-esports-sponsorships/

Red Bull, Why Spectating Can Make or Break a New Esport, November 2017, https://www.redbull.com/ca-en/spectating-esports-titles-accessibility

Venture Beat, The Future of Esports Marketing, November 2017
https://venturebeat.com/2017/11/09/the-future-of-esports-marketing-2/

Tech Crunch, Why Professional Sports Teams are Buying Esports Teams, September 2017

https://techcrunch.com/2017/09/20/heres-why-professional-sports-teams-are-buying-esports-teams/

ESPN Esports News, http://www.espn.co.uk/esports/

Esports Earnings, www.esportsearnings.com

IGN Esports News, http://uk.ign.com/events/esports

Esports Observer, https://esportsobserver.com/

Esports Insider, www.esportsinsider.com

Esports News UK, www.esports-news.co.uk

The Guardian, Esports News, https://www.theguardian.com/sport/esports

Kotaku Esports News, https://kotaku.com/tag/esports

Sky Sports Esports News, http://www.skysports.com/esports

61693310R00135

Made in the USA
Middletown, DE
13 January 2018